THE TRUTH ► IS IN THE ◄ TRIANGLE

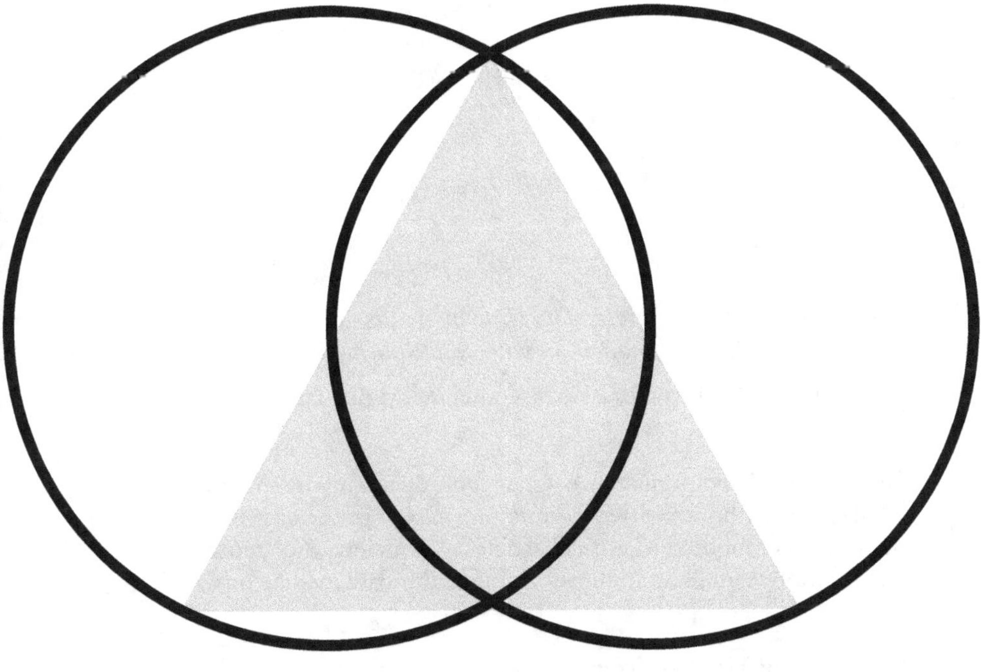

Published by Mindstir Media, LLC
45 Lafayette Rd | Suite 181 | North Hampton, NH 03862 | USA
1.800.767.0531 | www.mindstirmedia.com

Printed in the United States of America
ISBN-13: 979-8-9856345-9-4

THE TRUTH

▶ IS IN THE ◀

TRIANGLE

THE HIDDEN TRUTHS ON HOW TO ACHIEVE WHOLENESS IN YOUR RELATIONSHIPS

DR. FRANCES YAHIA

CONTENTS

▶ CHAPTER 1 ◀

RULES OF THE GAME

"Keep your eyes wide open before marriage, half shut afterwards."

~ Benjamin Franklin

Why, Why, Why!?

The purpose of this manual is to explain why all relationships begin, why all relationships have conflict, how to establish rules in a relationship, and how to renegotiate when "the original script" is no longer working for the couple so that the partnership will continue and will be stronger and healthier than before.

THE RULES OF RELATIONSHIP

Every relationship has rules, whether they are spoken or unspoken. And just as every relationship has rules, every therapeutic model has rules. In order to use this workbook, you must know and follow the rules of this particular model that I have devised. It's rooted in metaphysical principles and universal laws that have been extrapolated for modern-day application. The model works because these universal laws represent the truth of the spiritual and material world and, whether we have knowledge of them or not, we are held to their principles.

EVERYTHING IS A SYSTEM

A relationship is a system. Let's quantify this system and say it symbolizes 100 percent of your relationship with your partner or significant other. In other words, everything you do with each other can be registered on a scale of 0 to 100. For example, if you do 75 percent of the chores, your spouse is going to do 25 percent. If you do 90 percent, your spouse is going to do 10 percent. If you do 100 percent, he's going to sit on the couch with a beer. So don't give that much. Leave room for the laundry to be done.

And so it is with all of the actions and interactions we have with our partner. The most optimal partnership is one in which each individual in the couple operates at 50 percent.

The relationship system is what I call "a snow globe." Every system (relationship) has an origin story, the beginning of how it started. How you met your partner reflects your origin story. This system, this snow globe, has a crack in it. Why? Because it's been designed to shatter every five to seven years. If you examine the dynamics of each fight you have with your partner you will find that they link back to the relationship's initial origin story and your first fight.

This "creation myth" (origin story) will repeatedly fracture the system until the system either cracks completely or is re-established. This is when you're allowed to renegotiate the origin story of your relationship if you choose to. Some people choose not to renegotiate, and for years they harbor issues they've never discussed or examined. They're passive-aggressive, they're codependent, they don't go to therapy. Others, on the other hand, *want* to shatter that snow globe and reestablish the dynamics of their relationship based on a new origin story, on a new construct. They do the work—and they reap the rewards.

In examining the snow globe, we also need to look at what I call the "attachment style" inherent in the relationship. This is the basis of how we interact with our partner. According to developmental psychologists John Bowlby & Mary Ainsworth, there are secure attachment and insecure attachment styles. I am a believer that we only have insecure attachment styles because our security needs were not met in childhood. This model is to help us, as adults, develop secure attachment styles with ourselves by meeting our own needs and providing unconditional love to ourselves (the "I"), and in turn creating a secure attachment with our partner (the "WE"). A related function of the crack in the snow globe is to shatter your attachment style so that a new, more secure attachment style may replace it. A secure attachment style, as we get older and reach adulthood, is one where we are comfortable and happy with who we are and who we are becoming. In this, we are increasingly less dependent on our partner to meet our needs. Instead, we have learned the true function of our partner, and how to get most of our needs met independently of them.

We Inherited the Template

We, like everyone else, were given the template of the cracked system growing up, and whether we know it or not we're trying not to repeat the patterns we inherited, although most of us fail miserably at this. Let's use the analogy of the fairy tale "Snow White" to illustrate this point.

Snow White was the picture of innocence: virginal and beautiful. She lived in a cottage in the forest with the seven dwarfs, who were very protective of her and told her never to open the door to strangers. One day, when the trolls were out mining for gold in the mountains, there was a knock at the door. Snow White, despite the admonition of the trolls, opened it. She was faced by the evil queen who had been trying to do Snow White in. When she offered Snow White a bite of a delicious-looking apple, Snow White couldn't refuse. She partook of what was a poison apple and fell into a coma, which the dwarves discovered upon their return.

Snow White represents the innocence and trust of the early days of a relationship, before there is any disagreement or conflict. Snow White is also symbolized by the untainted environment of a snow globe before there are any cracks in it. But then the evil queen shows up and gives Snow White the poison apple to eat. The apple represents desire and when it's cut in half, the design of a pentagon—a pagan symbol—is revealed. The pentagon is a symbol of initiation, a symbol of volatility, of will, of desire, of wanting change.

We are Snow White and the snow globe is our environment before our first conflict with our partner, before our first fight. We then symbolically bite the apple so that we may enter into conflict and in so doing, hopefully deconstruct our destructive behavioral patterning and integrate our darker parts, our shadow. I call these our "discarded parts." To be truly whole, we must collect these discarded parts and integrate them into our psyche.

Everything Is a Mirror

The first step in integrating our discarded parts is to realize that everything is a mirror for us. Not only that, but we have chosen to partner with someone who not only sees our discarded parts but actually embodies the same discarded parts. Don't discard any parts, for all of them are useful.

Again, everything in our system is a mirror and our system is the snow globe.

Your partner's job is to mirror your discarded parts back to you. If your partner is modeling or mirroring to you a behavior that you dislike, that is the exact behavior that you need to integrate into your shadow. This can be a hard pill to swallow.

Don't look at it like this person is against you. You brought them into your system, into your snow globe, because they have the same discarded parts that you do and they're simply mirroring to you how to achieve self-love—for your relationship with your partner is really just an extension of your inner spiritual state.

If you participate in individual therapy or marriage counseling, you see the same thing. Many relationships end and that's okay. Change is a part of growth. What we can do, however, when we're still in relationship with that person, is to use them to extract whatever lesson(s) they are trying to teach us, what I call "milking the moment." Don't discard the relationship until you've done this! Don't let the experience (and the lesson embedded in the experience) go to waste! Use it as a teachable moment. If you have to get out quickly, once you're safe and settled, look back at what this relationship was mirroring about your shadow. Don't let the experience (and the lesson embedded in the experience) go to waste! Use it as a teachable moment.

After you've done that—after you've examined the lesson and hopefully learned something from it—when your relationship has taken its last breath, kick it to the curb and find another guy or girl. And remember: We create everything in our world. I am a believer that the psyche creates every situation so that we may extract its essence and learn from it—and this mirroring construct is no exception.

The Snow Globe of Illusion and the Crack

How quickly we fall for someone the minute they see our discarded parts. We call it love. That's why I ask, "How did you meet? Tell me the fantasy. What did he or she see in you?" They then tell me everything about the system and their snow globe.

The intact snow globe before it shatters. This is based on how you and your partner met and before the first fight.

When I ask them, "What was your first fight?" I am trying to identify the crack in the snow globe, for this is where my work as a therapist begins. The answer to this question tells me what I need to know about their needs for validation, how strong or weak their ego is, what their conflict style is, and whether or not they were "heard" when they had their first fight. This material informs the entire relationship and indeed, is the crux of it.

*The glyph of the planet mars representing the god Arēs
and the couple's first fight.*

The crack in the system represents opportunity. Aries in mythology is the god of war and represents the crack, the conflict. However, his energy is also considered to be creative energy in that Aries wants us to create a new foundation, a new snow globe with a really solid story, not a Hallmark fantasy. Let's renegotiate on a higher level of consciousness instead of engaging in passive-aggressive fighting. What happens when we cop out of doing this instead of addressing the real reason behind the conflict? We find codependent mechanisms with one another, or we find addictions to hide behind.

Often we default to a very low level of consciousness. In this, we fight, we yell, we stamp our feet, trying to get our needs met. Everybody has needs pertaining to safety, security, protection, validation, and love, and every single one of us is trying to see to it that our needs are validated and met. How can we channel that same "first fight" archetype, that same energy, that same crack, but at a higher level of consciousness?

You're not fighting with this person for no reason; you're fighting *for* something. You're fighting to get your needs met because you didn't have them met, or didn't have them sufficiently met, when you were a child. As an adult we enter into a relationship in order to hopefully, finally get these needs met. That's the snow globe. That's where your potential partner "sees" you. They "recognize" you. They "get" you. They see your discarded parts and they love you nonetheless. If both partners are conscious and work on building a firm foundation of the relationship *consciously*, everybody wins.

Let's next discuss how our parents impacted our creation story, for they have a lot more influence than we might think.

Your Partner = Your Parent

The word *parent* has the same letters as the word *partner*, except *partner* has an extra *R* (which, to my mind, stands for "redo"). The dynamics of your family as you were growing up are going to be manifested in the relationship you create when you're an adult—either that or you will manifest the opposite behavior. For example, if your mother stayed home and tended house and you swore you'd be nothing like her because she had no power or money,[1] you as an adult made working a priority and as a result, you were promoted to the position of manager, and neglected your domestic responsibilities—all in the name of doing things differently from your mother. However, your behavior symbolizes the exact same thing, for the Principle of Polarity states "all truths are but half-truths." She was practicing one extreme; you are practicing the other. Same coin, different side. Your adult relationship with your partner is an opportunity to redo these dynamics; to rewrite the original script that was imprinted on you when you were a child.

---

1 We can examine your mother's experience of making domestic life her priority using the 0 – 100 scale that I referenced at the beginning of this chapter. However, in this case we are examining the balance between her domestic life and her professional life, the latter of which she didn't have. In this instance we can say that her domestic life was 100 percent (of her life's experience) and her professional life was 0 percent (of her life's experience). The goal is to achieve self-mastery by living in the range of 48 – 52 in all things, both by balancing the demands of our own lives and also in relationship with our partner. Conflicts in the range of 8-10 tend to exemplify 0-100 swings and keep us in child mode asking others to meet our needs or love us unconditionally.

This is true even if the partner you are with now turns out *not* to be your life partner. But for the time that you're together, you are meant to try and achieve self-love—or aspects of it—and integrate the light and dark aspects of your shadow (more on this later).

Again, milk the experience. Don't let a relationship—as short-lived as it may be—get away from you. It's not written anywhere that we have to stay with the same person forever. We can outgrow people because we've learned a certain amount of self-love from them. The next person that we choose to couple up with will hopefully do for us what our former partner wouldn't or couldn't. No one person is going to teach us everything.

Extract the essence and milk the experience so that you can do your inner work. If you strip away the intimacy that you enjoy with your current partner, and really examine that person, you will recognize your mother or father. Ninety-nine percent of the time the parent that is reflected back at you is going to be the parent whose behavior you have not yet integrated.

How does the unintegrated parent show up in your relationship? They become every person, place, thing, and situation in your world that upsets you. You put your projections onto all these things and the prism for so doing is the unintegrated parent. This will show up in every fight and every vice—it's going to show up in everything that makes you feel like you are not a priority for your partner.

The Astrological Chart Is an Indicator

We can look to our natal astrological chart for guidance here. Specifically, whatever sign is on the cusp of your seventh house (the descendant) will reveal to you, in a nutshell, the imprint that both of your parents had on you. The archetype or pattern of this sign is probably somewhat of a secret in the family. Your parents built their relationship on this theme and we, their children, are destined to repeat it. That it appears on the cusp of the seventh house is significant in that this is the place where the sun set on the day of your birth. It is a part of our psyche that doesn't receive light until we work through it.

Here's an example. I have Gemini on the cusp of my seventh house. This tells me that my parents built their relationship on needs for validation and financial success, both of which are linked to Gemini and its ruling planet, Mercury. In my relationships, until I raised my consciousness, I thought my only worth was to provide money to my partner because I had learned from my parents' relationship that money was the currency of love.

In the Bible it says we are punished for the sins of the father. The reason we are in a relationship is so that we can work through and not repeat the dynamics and behavioral patterns of our mother and father's relationship. Part of our job as parents is to do things differently than our parents did. Most coupled individuals, however, rarely achieve this, in large part because we are too wounded ourselves.

In my book, *The Seven Gates: Seven Steps Beyond Self-Awareness,* I discuss "the band-AID" approach to the scarification of wounds. We don't ever fully heal our wounds—they are always there—but we *can* create a scar over them so that they no longer own us. The *AID* syllable of the band-AID approach stands for 1) Awareness, 2) Integration and 3) Doing things differently.

Initially we become aware of our issues. But because knowledge doesn't necessarily translate to behavior change, we have to integrate what our parents had to teach us. If we don't "integrate our parents," we're stuck holding the bag, doomed to repeat their mistakes again and again and again (there will be more on this later). This is what we call "transgenerational trauma" or "ancestral trauma."

If we can recognize that we're doing this we need to take the next step and do things differently (#doitdifferently). We don't react by manifesting the opposite behavior, for that's essentially repeating the same misguided behavior. Instead, we need to find the behavioral midpoint whereby we attain equilibrium and don't react unconsciously but respond consciously. This is what I call "living in the 48 – 52."

What does this "48 – 52" mean? I mentioned it a little earlier in this chapter, but let's now look a little more closely at this construct. In the course of any given day we are thrust into situations where we are an active participant. Just by virtue of the fact that we are social creatures dealing and interacting with other social creatures on a daily basis means we run the risk of having our buttons pushed, or otherwise getting triggered in some way. When this happens, our behavior may escalate and we may retaliate in kind, which is the last thing that we want to do.

When triggered, quantify your reaction on a scale of 0 – 100. We want our reaction to be in the middle zone, not too heated, not too removed. If we lash out at the person who has pushed our buttons, we are not operating in the 48 – 52 range, but more in the 90 or 95 range (because our response can be deemed to be inappropriately extreme). If, on the other hand, we step back, breathe deeply, and then calmly address the offending party, we could be said to be operating in the behavioral range of 48 – 52. This is where we want to be at all times and in every situation in order to generate inner peace.

Ancient philosophies understood this. For example, the Tao is a way of life that avoids extremes. Buddhism is another. When we look to the Yin-Yang, the objective is to stay in the middle of the symbol, the curved line. The same is true for Tai Chi wherein the path between any extremes passes through a middle way, a compromise. In Aristotle's Nicomachean Ethics there is a golden mean between the extremes.

If we can stay in the 48 – 52 we can find balance and equanimity 24/7. What is equanimity? It's the state of inner calm and composure that prevails internally no matter what is happening externally.

All of this is about self-mastery, which is the goal of life. If we can achieve this equanimity, despite the myriad limitations that we face as spiritual beings having a human experience, then we can master life.

▶ CHAPTER 2 ◀

MYTHOLOGY, THE HIEROS GAMOS, AND THE VESICA PISCIS

"To say that one waits a lifetime for his soulmate to come around is a paradox. People eventually get sick of waiting, take a chance on someone, and by the art of commitment become soulmates, which takes a lifetime to perfect."

~ Criss Jami, American poet, philosopher, and songwriter

THERE ARE NO NEW STORIES

We can learn a lot if we understand how the ancients dealt with the metaphysical matters that concern us in this book. In this we can look to the world of myth for guidance. The myth that I want to share with you now is that of Zeus and Hera.

Zeus was the king of Olympus, the god of the Upper World. When the world was divided, Zeus got the biggest piece, the heavens. He married Hera. This union symbolizes the way marriage is supposed to be. That said, their union wasn't perfect, but our model stems from this mythology. Zeus is a whore: he cheats on Hera with men, women, and animals; he cannot keep it in his pants. That's going to play a role in what I call "the mistress" (and every relationship has a mistress; I explore this further in my podcast "Mistress of the Subconscious," which is available as an Apple podcast).

With Hera we have the archetype of the suspicious wife. She's constantly checking Zeus's phone, checking his email, finding out where he's going, who he's with, how he's betraying her, and so on and so forth. All couples are not the same but may have elements of their relationship that are similar to the construct of the nagging, controlling wife, or that of the husband who is sleeping with the housekeeper. These stereotypes that we see in cinema and books come from this mythology of Zeus and Hera.

Zeus and Hera have two children. This is really important: from marriage, two things are born. First of all, we have Hephaestus, the God of the Forge, who is deformed. When Hera looks at Hephaestus, she's sick to her stomach. She says to him, "You're not my kid, you're gross and deformed," and throws him to the bottom of the ocean so that the nymphs can raise him. Hephaestus is discarded, and as such, represents what's outdated or "wrong" in ourselves. Hephaestus also represents escapism, the snow globe, innocence, fantasy, addiction, martyrdom, rescue, and the victim mentality. However, he also symbolizes spirituality and wholeness. Hephaestus is an innocent, and that's going to be important as well.

Between the moment of our birth and the age of seven (what I call the "0 – 7"), most of us were given the message that we were not enough, that we were not worthy. We were not accepted for ourselves and this created our own particular story, our own personal mythology.

Hera and Zeus's second child was Aries, the God of War. Aries is the favorite son of Zeus and Hera, specifically Hera. He is the warrior. He is the archetype of war—the brute of war—and as such represents battle and conflict. Despite this, he also has a creator energy. So clearly there is not only conflict here, but a positive side as well. All archetypes have light and dark. The light side is the creator side—the ability to create something new.

This something new is self-love.

Your main goal of being with your partner is to achieve is self-love. The purpose, the be-all and end-all of your relationship, why you got married, why you had children, or why you built a business, whatever your thing was, is for you to learn self-love. It's for you to heal your own childhood snow globe. In this you are able to reconnect your discarded parts that your lover—luckily enough—sees and mirrors and models back to you so that you can integrate those parts of yourself that have been discarded (if you know how to work the system).

I have to learn about me and love me and heal my snow globe, my wounds, before I can do anything for another person. We have to understand this. This is the part of establishing and maintaining healthy boundaries; this is germane to understanding that you are an "I" before you're a "WE", and cannot sacrifice your "I" for the "WE".

THE I, THE I & THE WE

In mythology we have the Hephaestus-Aries-Aphrodite triangle in which Aphrodite was married to Hephaestus and was having sex with Aries. The reason that Aphrodite is the wife and the lover of both Aries and Hephaestus is that we need both aspects (erotic love and agape love) integrated within ourselves in order to achieve self-love. Once we have accomplished this, we are finally capable of generating real love that we can give to our partner in a mature, appropriate, and conscious fashion.

SOULMATE VERSUS THREADMATE

Before introducing our next talking points, which are the Vesica Piscis and the Hieros Gamos, I'd like to introduce an important idea that will have a bearing on all future discussions in this book. The concept is that of the *threadmate*, and it contrasts with the new age term *soulmate*. People believe that there's one particular person out there for them to partner up with and this one person is deemed to be a soulmate. This is actually a little misguided. A "soulmate" from a new age perspective can be any one of a number of people who vibrate at your energetic level.

Think of a ladder, the rungs of which range from A to Z. If you're vibrating energetically at the letter D, there are many people in your world who can vibrate at the same level (letter), not just one. To cut through the confusion, I've renamed *soulmate* to call it *threadmate*. Threadmates pair up according to shared values and whether or not they vibrate at the same level, which is reflective of another metaphysical law called the Principle of Vibration.

While we understand there are several partners for each person, we choose our partner at any given time to fulfill a common goal that we've decided upon together before incarnation.

You may have many threadmates during the course of your life based on the many things you have set out to accomplish before being birthed into this world. There are many steps to making a threadmate relationship really work. I cover this in greater detail in my book *Hidden Truths: The Magic of Mysticism and Its Modern-Day Applications.*

THE I, THE I & THE WE

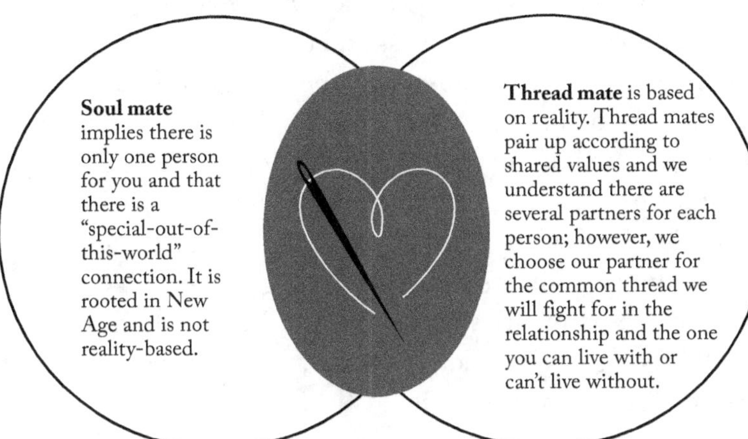

MYSTICISM OF RELATIONSHIPS: THE CIRCLE, THE VESICA PISCIS, AND THE HIEROS GAMOS

Now we can move on to the circle, the Vesica Piscis, and the *Hieros Gamos* (a term that means "mystical marriage"). The symbolism of the circle is what we call "sacred geometry." The circle is never ending and nonhierarchical and all spiritual traditions and philosophies are centered around it. From it all other sacred geometrical figures are formed. The squared circle represents another image of sacred geometry involving the circle.

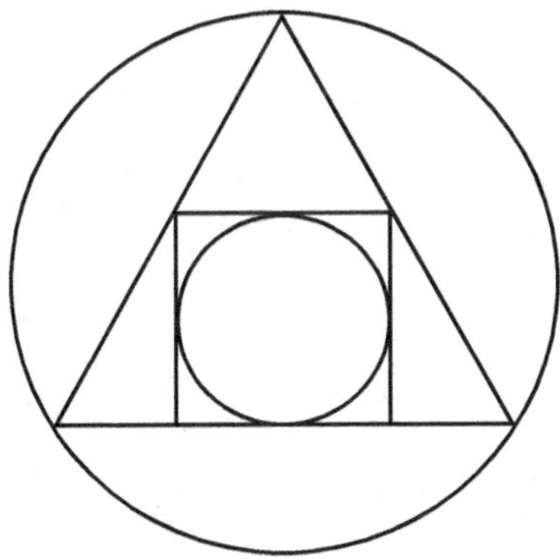

The Squared Circle

The circle represents wholeness and the entire universe; however, the triangle represents the thoughts that keep us separate from that universal consciousness and the square is the boundaries we set up to keep us from observing the thoughts. The inner circle represents the divine spark we have inside. The Truth is in the Triangle because it is our thoughts and judgements about our partner that keep us in conflict and setting up unnecessary boundaries to stay safe. In this model we have a constant inventory of the thoughts and judgements about everything we don't like about our partner so the boundaries and walls that keep us fighting breakdown. With higher vibration thoughts, we create boundaries that keep our "I" intact, but keep the "WE" flowing.

From the circle we build the Vesica Piscis, which is another figure from sacred geometry. It features two interlocking circles. The Vesica Piscis is the symbol for what I call "the I-I-WE." The "I-I-WE" is the construct that two individuals must first be whole unto themselves before coming into conscious union with one another. Or they can create this wholeness by the work they do during the relationship, through the art and skill of renegotiating with their partner.

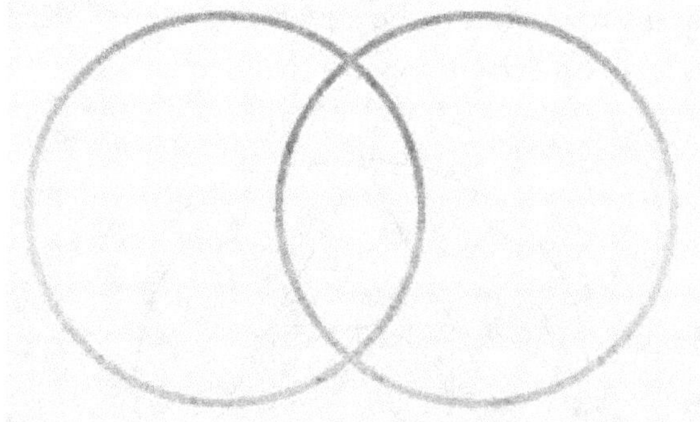

The Vesica Piscis

In this image of the Vesica Piscis the overlapping circles represent the two individuals in the relationship (the two I's) and the center oval, known as the mandorla, represents the relationship as its own entity, the "WE" of it all. The "WE" only holds one thread, one need per partner and one non-negotiable per partner so it is smaller than the "I" circles. When you are whole in your "I" you can make the relationship a part of you, not the entirety of who you are. Make no mistake about it, your relationship is an actual entity. It is a child. It is a creation and it has its own creation myth and origin story.

In creating this "relationship" each partner brings 48 – 52 percent of their whole self to the new entity but doesn't lose themselves in the process. Relationships are the fastest way to enlightenment because your partner is mirroring your shadow (unintegrated parent) constantly and when we use this continuous flow of information to identify that we are the same as what we are judging in our thoughts about our partner (and parent), we raise consciousness. If they've lost themselves in the process because they haven't done the necessary inner work on themselves, I will work with them, as their therapist, to restore the "I" part of the "I-I-WE" equation (this is *The Seven Gates* model). When they end up in counseling to work on the relationship, not only do we address the relationship, I also encourage them to examine their own issues, irrespective of their partner, at the same time—to work on themselves *and* the relationship. If they are successful, they will have attained the Hieros Gamos.

The Hieros Gamos tradition derives from antiquity wherein a woman would marry her godhead of choice (symbolically). The god would often be represented by a statue, and as such, would be featured in a ceremony whereby the woman and her god would marry in a "mystical marriage." The godhead could be said to represent the divine nature of the individual whereas the woman represents the earthly nature of the individual. The result of the "marriage" would be a divine union. A mystical marriage is the concept of marrying both our divine aspects with our flawed, earthly aspects.

The ancient metaphysical law, the Principle of Gender, reflects this Hieros Gamos tradition, which I have expanded to apply to human relationships today. For those of you who would like more on this subject, please refer to my book *Witch Bitch* for the Hieros Gamos ceremony.

The Hieros Gamos is discussed in many spiritual texts and often includes information about tantric practices that are associated with it. These practices may be sexual in nature, for many spiritual texts point to the association between Spirit and sexuality wherein the second chakra, the shiva shakti, the lingam, and the yoni all have important roles to play.

The MFC Triad

My first book and therapeutic model, *The Seven Gates*, is about bringing yourself to wholeness and understanding your subconscious wounds—how they were created at the moment of your conception (your creation myth) and how they prevailed throughout your mother's pregnancy, through your birth process, and up through the age of seven (the 0 – 7). These first seven years of life created your personal mythology, with the people, the attitudes, and the narratives that you will build your life upon.

My model, the "Truth is in the Triangle" examines our most intimate relationships and teaches us how to work through and heal our subconscious traumas. This construct necessitates that you've already done some work unveiling the traumatic events buried in your subconscious, you're assuming a relationship with someone else who's done *their* work, and together you're now forming, or attempting to form, the Hieros Gamos.

In building the third unit, the "WE," strong adult principles should be consciously incorporated into your relationship so that the relationship may move forward in a healthy way. The first step is to define your relationship *thread*, and then to determine what I call the "non-negotiables" attendant to that thread. I will walk you through this now.

Define Your Relationship Thread

You can't have a healthy "I-I-WE" (Hieros Gamos) if you don't know what your thread is. Your thread is your shared value system. If you're unaware of your values, you have no direction of what you're working toward. Why did you come together? There is no wrong answer, but you need to agree on this. Write what the shared value is on the threadmate worksheet (found in the workbook in the appendix to this book). What is the thread that you have with this person? Why did you get together? Was it for sex? Money? To piss off your parents? To have a baby? It really doesn't matter what the thread is, but every relationship needs to have one and it must be defined at the outset of the relationship.

What is your thread?

I had a client who asked me, "How do I build my 'I-I-WE'?" I asked her, "Well, what's your thread?"

She told me it was her family. She has a family, he has a family, and the "WE" she wants the thread to be is the shared family—all of them together. Although she and her partner may not have kids together, they're definitely blended, and that's where the "WE" comes in.

This primary thread can be renegotiated every five to seven years (which I'll discuss later). This is important. If you have a couple who gets together for the thread of building a business, and one of them cheats by having an affair, if the thread is otherwise intact this should not be a deal-breaker or a non-negotiable. If your thread is to build a business, and the business is successful, why are you looking at the infidelity? If this should happen to you, try and look at it as a learning experience to see what you need to integrate. But again, there's no need to get divorced given that you have not deviated from your thread's purpose. The purpose of the thread is to remind you the function of the relationship. If the conflict that arises doesn't lead you back to the thread it's an issue to take up in the "I" not the "We". The one need and one non-negotiable provide the healthy boundaries (square) the relationship needs, if not everything but the kitchen sink will become a problem. The conflict or judgement is the thought (triangle) and keeps us from our wholeness and that wholeness with our partner (circle) because we want to remember subconsciously that our parents discarded us and are projecting that on to our partner. Get very clear on your thread, as this will be the primary connection you share with your partner for 5 to 7 years.

Besides sex, couples should identify one specific unmet need they want their partner to fulfill. That's it. You and your partner only need to define one thread between the two of you, one unmet need each and one-non-negotiable each. Any conflict that arises that is not linked to the thread is off limits to the "WE" and the couple, each respective partner needs to return to their "I" and identify what is being brought up for them from their childhood and their shadow. This keeps the 48-52 intact. If you don't understand the thread—the shared values upon which you built the relationship—then you run the risk of being in conflict unnecessarily. Again, this is about clarity, about getting clear about what the focus of the relationship should be. The thread indicates what need you and your partner are meeting in one another.

Determine the Non-Negotiables

As the next step after *identifying* your thread, you and your partner together need to define the non-negotiables of your thread. This will comprise the rule book of the relationship. In this, each partner lists the non-negotiables of their own individual "I"—one per person. This must be something that violates your core "I" values so deeply that you're willing to call it quits and walk away.

This is a contract that (usually for five to seven years also) articulates how you will build the relationship and hold each other accountable to the standards you decide upon together. In devising your non-negotiables, keep in mind that they should be aligned with the values of the thread itself. If your thread is to build a business, then the non-negotiable should correlate with the values of building a business. For instance, the non-negotiable might be that there is total transparency in all of the company's financial dealings. The relationship will end if these non-negotiables occur or, hypothetically for instance, if you spend 20 percent of the business's income without consulting the other. The non-negotiables are the ultimate things you will never accept. They are the deal-breakers and they are linked to your values. If you violate these, you're betraying yourself as well as your partner. That's why there should only be one or two deal-breakers maximum per person.

HIEROS GAMOS

Build the I-I-We.
What are the non-negotiables of each I and of the We?

Only articulate and decide upon rules or non-negotiables that pertain to your relationship thread. Take this important step at the start of your journey together. What are those non-negotiables? Together they will create the rule book for your relationship. In my first book, *The Seven Gates*, I asked readers to develop a rule book for *themselves* as individuals. In *this* book, it's your relationship that needs to be guided by rules. You *must* have non-negotiables. One person cannot meet all of your needs—that isn't the point of a relationship. However, that one person can meet one of your needs: the one linked to your common thread and its rules.

Your attempt to couple with another person is an attempt to shatter the snow globe of delusion derived from your childhood home and re-establish something new—to not repeat the sins of the father, to not repeat your parents' trauma in marriage. And it doesn't matter if you knew your parents or not, for your entire narrative was established at the moment of conception.

How exactly do we shatter the snow globe? We begin by installing better communication practices, stronger boundaries, and we integrate our dark bits. By evolving together with our partner in relationship in this conscious way, we also evolve with our children because our improvements in this arena mean that they themselves will have a healthier future.

And with that we can change the world.

▶ CHAPTER 3 ◀

LEAVE, LEARN, RETURN

"I love being married. It's great to find that one special person you want to annoy for the rest of your life."

~ Rita Rudner, Stand-Up Comedian

Each and every one of us is an integral part of a triangle comprised of the dynamics derived from our relationship with our mother, our father, and ourself. Given this, every single situation we encounter represents those dynamics derived from our mother and father. Further to this, we (metaphorically) "married" our mother or our father.

In *The Seven Gates* I explain that a woman and a man get together and have a child, you. The state of mind (consciousness, quality of thoughts) of your parents at your moment of conception became your subconscious programming. The competitive voice inside your head, one that you hear throughout your life, is derived from this programming, unless and until you decide to change it.

The subconscious programming is developed in four stages: 1) at the moment of conception; 2) during pregnancy, which adds an additional layer: how you choose to be loved both in healthy and unhealthy ways, which will definitely come up in your relationships; 3) it's reflected in your birth story, which is how you change and move into transitions throughout your life; 4) last, with the subconscious programming that you inherit from the age of 0–7, you access the backstory of the subconscious wounding your psyche is undergoing.

Up until the age of seven you develop this story—your personal mythology and your Hephaestus version of yourself. (To refresh, Hephaestus was the god who was thrown out of Olympus because he was deformed.) You will get into a relationship with someone who acknowledges your discarded parts and you will get together with your partner to help heal this aspect of Hephaestus within you both. This is when you figure out that there's something wrong with you (metaphorically). For instance, you're expelled from your family, you're kicked out of school, your brother was born and you are no longer the only child—whatever your "story" is, it was developed, and you were made aware of it, by the time you were seven years old.

That's your personal mythology and you're going to own it. As an adult you enter into a relationship and hopefully, you can then break your story down and rewrite a new version of it from a much healthier perspective. In this you will hopefully heal and help your partner heal as well, building your relationship anew.

The Mono Myth

Many myths contain the construct of the hero leaving "home." The great mythologist Joseph Campbell spoke of what is called a "mono myth" in which he identified that all mythologies showed that we must leave home, answer a call, figure something out, and then return home. It's the story of the prodigal son in the Bible, it's Demeter and Persephone in Greek mythology, it's Odysseus leaving to fight the Trojan War. Here "home" is not a physical place; home is within; it's a state of mind. Home is a metaphorical space within yourself. It's important to understand this.

I once had a client say, "I don't have a home." What I heard is that they don't have any inner peace. They're not centered. They don't really have a true identity, a true sense of self with a capital *S*. Part of the mystical marriage and why we marry this god or goddess in ceremony is because we're trying to unify the external universe with our internal self.

This is reflected in the Principle of Correspondence, which I discuss at length in my book *Hidden Truths: The Magic of Mysticism and Its Modern-Day Applications*. The Principle of Correspondence adheres to the ancient maxim "As above, so below, as within, so without." This principle embodies the truth that there is always a correspondence between the laws and phenomena of the various planes of being and real life as we live it every day.

Your internal state reflects your external circumstances and your home state is inside, where you feel at peace and centered, your third chakra. When you "come home" to yourself in this way, you may be once again in the same environment that you "left"—but something is not the same. Your state of mind has changed. Your own sense of Self has changed. A Zen maxim reflects this: "Before enlightenment, chop wood, carry water. After enlightenment, chop wood, carry water." Again, the external circumstances have not changed but inside you are different.

You've grown up, so to speak. That's the "adult" in *The Seven Gates*. You left the "child," a state of mind that's all about meeting your parents' needs and being part of a unit that may not have a shared value system anymore. However, although you may leave your parents' value system, you don't veer too far away from it. You also don't ask them to meet your needs anymore as your values have shifted. When you "return home" as the adult you've learned how to meet your own needs rather than expecting your partner or anyone else to meet your needs for you.

Again, we have to leave home in order to come back to ourselves. We chop wood, become enlightened, and then chop wood again. We're back in the same house, with the same people, we're in the same marriage, the same job. Nothing on the outside looks to have changed because this is an inner process, like the chrysalis that transmutes when it hatches a butterfly from a caterpillar. What's changed is your inner cocoon, your state of mind, your state of consciousness—that's the mystical marriage.

Transmutation is the only way to raise consciousness and is the purpose of your lifetime and the relationships that fill it.

You will not change the state of mind that has been with you from conception—what we call the "Manas Prakriti" in Ayurveda. The manas prakriti is simply the breakdown of how much male energy and female energy you have. People with a lot of fire and air are more energetically masculine and water and earth people are more energetically feminine. An easy way to calculate this is with your astrological chart. Every planet has an air, fire, earth or water sign. You can add them up and get a rough idea of your elemental breakdown; however, your power currency, which I'll discuss below is another way to know. This has nothing to do with sex, gender or sexuality, it is linked to the power currency we prefer generally. Overt power tends to be linked to more fire and air and covert power tends to be linked to people with more earth and water. Your manas prakriti, elements or power currency cannot determine your level of consciousness. That is based on free will. However, you can and hopefully will change your state of consciousness from a lower level of consciousness to a higher level of consciousness. The next step is to replicate this same evolution in your relationship with your partner.

Power Currency

When your parents were deciding how they were going to be a couple in the world, you were taking an inventory of how they interacted with each other. As part of their determination, they negotiated and maintained a specific power currency between themselves. You stood back and studied their behaviors, your subconscious recording it all.

There are two types of power currency: overt power and covert power. Overt power implies aggression or violence. It can also manifest as the partner who makes the money or otherwise controls the purse strings of the household. Covert power, on the other hand, implies manipulation and passive-aggression and it may manifest in behavior such as being overly submissive, muttering under one's breath, or plotting revenge.

As a child you looked at your parents, and you asked yourself, "Who has the power here?"

Subconsciously at that point you decided which parent had the power currency *you* preferred: covert or overt. One modality is not necessarily better than the other; again, whichever one you choose just represents a subconscious decision you made about how you too were going to move through the world.

The parent who has the same power currency you do is the parent you have the wrong alliance with. I call it "wrong alliance" because we shouldn't be in alliance with our parents. Our parents made an alliance between themselves and you, the child, should crown that alliance in the way that you were told it was supposed to be, but wasn't for any of us. No child has been loved unconditionally or had their needs met. This is why we are all symbolically Hephaestus.

As we've established, every single person on the planet is involved in the triangular dynamics of mother, father, and child. The ideal triangle would be your mother and your father (represented by Zeus and Hera) at the base of the triangle, and you (represented by Hephaestus or Aries) at the tip of it. Your parents are the base, the foundation, and you're the product of their alliance.

That would be the healthy model. However, this typically is not the case.

Instead, the parent who you have the wrong alliance with is at the bottom of the triangle, and the other parent is at its tip. Again, the parent who you have the wrong alliance with is the one whose style (or currency) of power you preferred—even if you never met them! And please understand that when I'm referring to your "parents" here I'm referring to the subconscious programming that you inherited from them. If you did not know your parents, you were adopted, you were a test tube baby and so on . . . your thought processes and the quality of those thoughts will still reflect these parents and an alliance to one of them.

WRONG & RIGHT ALLIANCES

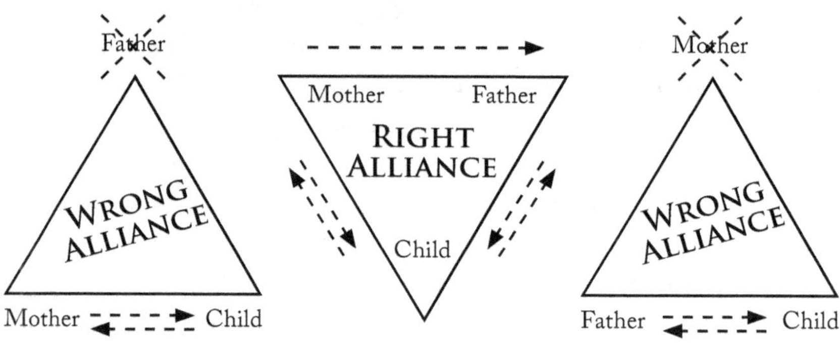

Your alliance will probably align with the parent whose communication style you admired and wanted to replicate. Your father may have had the money and called the shots, your mother may might have been a bit manipulative. Your father's power currency was overt; your mother's covert. You liked that overt sense of power and you subconsciously told yourself that you were going to model it. And that's how you became. One of the results is that you had a wrong alliance with your father.

That's what happened to me.

In my case, my dad had more overt power than my mother did, and he communicated in a way that was in keeping with this. I obviously liked that, and I chose to follow in his footsteps and live out my relationships that same way. You may think your alliance is with your mother because you go shopping and gossip. Or you might play golf with your father and get along just fine. However, your alliance has nothing to do with the personal relationship you had or did not have with a particular parent.

It's also true that the partner you attract is going to have the power currency of the other parent—the one you do *not* have the wrong alliance with (the unintegrated parent, what I call the "bad buckets"). This is the parent at the tip of the triangle. In this case, given that the father's power currency is preferred, that would be the mother. Given that your partner will share the same covert power currency as your mother, he no doubt will prefer a nice-guy mask and show up in life as a sheep, a martyr, or a victim.

I had a client who worked at a plastic surgeon's office and she would tell potential clients to first have sex with their husbands and then ask them for the money for surgery. That's a covert power play. Nothing new. Then you've got the woman in the boardroom who unbuttons her blouse and shows her boobs to the boss. That's an overt power play.

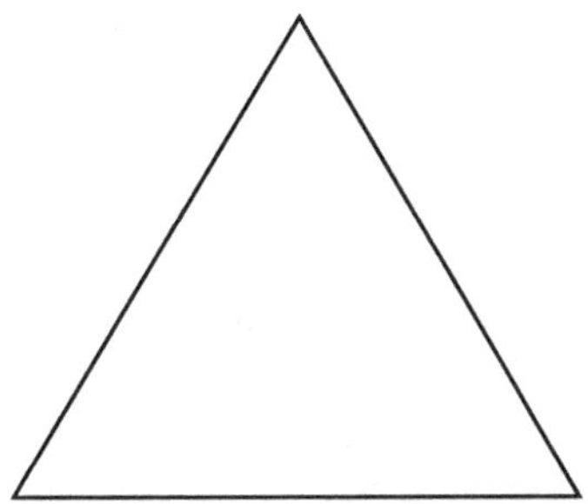

Who is your wrong alliance with?
Which parent needs to be integrated?

So, which one are you? Are you the covert power player or the overt power player? Who had the covert and the overt power in your parents' relationship? The bottom line is it's the same thing, the same coin. However, it dictates how you show up in the world, what you need to integrate, and the partner you will attract.

So chose the power currency you like best. It's like in the film *My Big Fat Greek Wedding*, when the mother says to the daughter,

"Your father's the head, but I'm the neck." Are you the head or the neck? That's another way to ask which power currency you prefer, overt or covert. Which one are you? Which one do you like to be? Are you the main event or are you the back-up singer? Which one of your parents had more power? Again, there's no right or wrong answer here. This is just to determine which parent you have the wrong alliance with.

My client Marla once told me, "My mother, you know, is a good person, she's selfless."

I responded by saying, "That's an interesting choice of words," to which she replied, "Well, she is better than my father, who is a selfish bastard." What she was identifying with was the covert power currency of her mother versus the overt power style of her father.

People today seem to admire those who are "selfless." This isn't something that I necessarily agree with, as people who behave in a "selfless" manner often do so in order to gain the admiration of others. Instead, one should be able to give *to* oneself (not negate oneself), to get one's own needs met, and ensure that one isn't violating the rights of others in so doing.

Good Buckets, Bad Buckets

In my previous book *The Seven Gates*, I talk about "good buckets" and "bad buckets," which are the good qualities of your mother, the good qualities of your father, the bad qualities of your mother, the bad qualities of your father. But news flash! Your mother and your father are the same person—again, just different sides of the same coin! That's why you can't do things in the way that is opposite to the way that your unintegrated parent did because then you're doing the same thing: You're living at one extreme or the other. The difference is that one of your parents used covert power and one of them used overt power. They were mirrors of each other, just as you are a mirror of your partner. That is why from the birth of Zeus and Hera's marriage—conflict and power struggles (as represented by Aries)—emerged.

How do we make peace with all this? First identify which parent you have the wrong alliance with. Again, this will be the parent whose power currency, overt or covert, you admire the most. Once you draw your triangle and have identified that your father is your wrong alliance, you realize that your mother is on the triangle's tip. This is the exiled parent, the unintegrated parent with the different power currency.

Focusing on this exiled parent, determine what this parent (in this example the mother) showed you in the bad buckets that you've discarded as part of your shadow. Bring it in. Integrate it into your life so that from now on you can work from a place of wholeness. If you don't like your nose because it's just like your father's, would you cut it off? No! but somehow, we think we can discard our traits and behaviors, as if doing so won't hurt us or cause problems later on.

It is oftentimes through marriage that we make the subconscious or the bad buckets conscious and through our relationship we integrate what I call "the mistress" or the unintegrated parent. The relationship brings forth the exiled parent, with our spouse as the representative.

BAND-AID

Earlier I talked about the I-I-WE model and how we first have to be a fully developed "I" before we can enter into mature partnership as a "WE." If you're building your "I" and "WE" at the same time, you can use the Band-AID approach, the second syllable standing for, again: A: Awareness; I: Integration: D: Doing things differently (#doitdifferently). We use this Band-AID approach to become whole (the "I"), to heal the wound, or to affect as much healing as possible (by creating a scar over the wound).

From the moment of birth to the age of seven (the 0 – 7), your subconscious was developing and as such, was categorizing everything that your mother and father did and said as "good" or "bad." Remember, every person, place, thing, or situation is representative of your mother or father.

As you decided what went into the good and bad buckets, you developed your shadow. The bad buckets of your parents became your shadow and what you try to hide as you live your life. This is what I call FOFO, "fear of being found out." If you show these bad buckets, or shadow, to the world, you believe you will be discarded and deemed unworthy, just like Hephaestus was.

How do we apply this to ourselves? Make a list of the good and bad qualities of your parents, which you observed from 0 – 7 years of age. If you don't remember much of the 0 – 7 years, you can populate the buckets with more recent memories. Again, the bad buckets are whatever you didn't like about your parents. It also constitutes your shadow and what you don't like about yourself.

Now look at these bad buckets, in particular as they pertain to the parent at the tip of the triangle. While you are integrating that parent you may arrive at a different perception about what's good and bad because good and bad are relative constructs. There's no real "good" and there's no real "bad." There are universal truths, and there are value statements and judgments.

Again, there are very few universal truths. These labels you've decided are "good" and "bad" are half-truths, what you deem to be true—but you're judging yourself and others when you drag in this notion of truth. I always say that judgments are confessions and they're great because they tell me what you value in the bad buckets that you still haven't forgiven yourself for valuing; thereby, judging it in yourself and by default others. Judgements also tell me what you haven't integrated and accepted in yourself. For example, if I judge someone's appearance, I'm in essence judging my own vanity. Since my mother's bad bucket contained vanity and she's my outcast parent, every time I judge someone's appearance, I'm judging my own and I'm judging that I am vain and don't want to admit it yet. Many years ago, my husband and I had an argument about a new jacket he wanted to purchase before a weekend trip we were taking up North. I stated he already had a nice jacket and why would he need another one. I immediately went inward to shift the triangle, as this was merely a reflection of my own bad bucket and my mother. The more it shows up in my relationship, the more opportunities I have to work through it. Acceptance is loving myself despite being vain and being just like my mother, my shadow. This in essence is the mystical marriage, my divine nature and earthly flawed nature coexisting and creating a space for self-love within myself. As I use my partner's vanity to integrate my own shadow, I no longer have to cause conflict with him. Since vanity has nothing to do with our thread, I also know it is an "I" issue not a "WE" issue. This is the opposite side of the coin. What you're judging is linked to the bad buckets and the unintegrated parent (mistress) and is the key to your wholeness and your ability to live in truth.

Make the Invisible Visible

We now have to pick a side. We're required to do that. Each one of us must stand for something. Pick the qualities of the unintegrated parent and start choosing which of those bad bucket qualities you'll integrate. Part of the integration process of healing the subconscious is understanding that you have chosen the wrong alliance. Despite this, your present level of consciousness is derived from both of your parents and integrating both is the only way to be whole. At this point you may be saying, "Wait a minute, maybe my mother *does* have something to offer me after all and I'm going to integrate the contents of her bad bucket and find out."

Don't throw the baby out with the bathwater. Maybe your mother's bucket *does* have some wisdom in it. For instance, if your mother's bad bucket dictates that she's overly cautious all the time, maybe you will witness an incidence where this caution actually saved a life. Thus, you may come to decide that your mother is/was right to be this way after all. Caution is linked to covert power and is a control mechanism; therefore, this example says you don't value the covert power your mother had and you probably became impulsive and rash in order to not be like your mother. You are a scaredy-cat at the end of the day (cautious) but you don't want to be found out so you act abrasively and boldly in order to compensate.

In my example, my mother was very image oriented. She was beautiful and glamorous, and I tried to deny that I valued these qualities. Therefore, I developed an eating disorder, was overweight, and got breast cancer in an attempt to *not be her*. When I realized that I did value my image, and that I could integrate these qualities of my mother's and do things differently, I healed. It's important to clarify that you may live out your life pretending you do not have this quality or that quality and build your whole life around pretending you do not value it (that exact same quality), but you do.

The good news is that once you own this, you also realize that you can do things differently. Not making changes based on what you now know or pretending that the issue doesn't exist in the first place will not make it go away. It makes it stronger and as such, may destroy your life. It's the hydra head that you chop off and two grow back in its place.

I can tell you that both your parents have something to teach you—they have some wisdom to impart to you, even if you're adopted, even if they mistreated you. There is wisdom in those buckets, and if they reflect the quality of your own thoughts, you need to understand them in order to understand your own psyche. And the only way you're going to understand that is by populating those buckets and identifying that *you are them*. Rather than shunning the bad buckets/shadow and hating yourself for being your parents, or the parts that you don't like about them, you need to integrate them so that you become a whole person.

This goes back to the original Hieros Gamos, the mystical marriage between you and yourself. You've got to achieve Selfhood. You've got to achieve a place of home within—and that only comes from integrating those buckets that your mother and father gave you. Your partner is the unintegrated parent and again, is the reason why we enter into significant relationships in the first place—so that we may develop Selfhood.

Hopefully you don't repeat the same Zeus and Hera relationship that your parents had, and which most people have today. Again, doing the opposite is not doing it differently! So don't do that! Truly do things differently (don't be at either extreme), and you will find a healthy way to live in a relationship.

Every single one of you has had a relationship that has at times taken the energy or the focus off of you. That man or that woman preferred their friends, their drinks, their football, their kid—something. What took the energy off of you is the unintegrated parent. It is your mother or your father.

Here is an example from a client of mine: "My wife focused on work more than the partnership." So work is the issue.

Who focused more on work, mom or dad?

"Mom." So, the issue is the fact that the child didn't get the attention he needed from his mother, rather work got the mother's attention.

We will recreate this pattern over and over again until we realize that there is some "work" in our own lives that we need to be doing. And the reason we don't do it, the reason we leave this out is because we don't want to integrate that parent. Because what happens if you become your mother? What happens if you become your father? All of a sudden, you're saying "I'm just like my mom," "I'm just like my unintegrated parent." It's hard to accept that you're the unintegrated parent because that exact shadow is what you've built your life on hiding and pretending that you're not. It's also the exact same person you will attract in your life until you integrate it.

That (unintegrated) parent is the key to your healing. I don't know anyone who would wish this upon themselves, but in truth, identifying this and integrating it is the path of liberation.

CHAPTER 4

THE TIP OF THE TRIANGLE

"You don't love someone for their looks, or their clothes, or their fancy car, but because they sing a song only you can hear."

~ Oscar Wilde

Let's return now to the truth in the triangle. The tip of the triangle holds the truth of what you are not accepting that you need to accept and what your partner is trying to help you integrate. Remember, your partner is your parent and the tip of the triangle holds the truth about what you don't want to accept about yourself. I didn't want to accept that I was my mom, so I "married" my mom. If you finally accept this, you're admitting that you're that parent, you're integrating that shadow, and your partner is your parent. When we do this, we no longer require our partner to meet our needs because we begin meeting our own needs for ourselves.

The child part of you (Hephaestus) that was "discarded" is constantly seeking his or her needs to be met, all day long. It never stops! If you ate a piece of bread, you'd be satiated for a couple of hours, however, the subconscious unmet need (hunger) is never satiated. In your relationship it's expected that your partner will meet your needs. This strains relationships. When we get clear about what our needs actually are, we learn to meet them ourselves by integrating the shadow. This lightens the demands on our relationships and we can enjoy healthier partnerships as a result.

Your opportunity to reform your mother/father/child triad is in your relationship, what I call shifting the system or shifting the triangle. Have you been in a relationship where you or your partner cheated? Put that at the tip of your triangle. Who is the cheater? Your mother or your father? You can phrase the question who metaphorically cheated, mother or father, as the universe is not literal, it is symbolic. For example, did father cheat on his taxes or did mother cheat death in her car accident? When a conflict arises in your relationship create a conflict statement, sum up the conflict or issue in one sentence. For example, my husband doesn't take out the garbage and leaves me to do it and it makes me feel unheard. You can then extrapolate from the conflict statement and ask "which parent made you feel unheard", mother or father? This is also an opportunity to revisit the thread. Is feeling heard tied to the thread or the unmet need or non-negotiable? If not, go into your "I" rather than bringing it to the "WE."

Here's an example from my own practice.

I had a couple as clients and he cheated on her; we will call them James and Rebecca. I put "infidelity" at the tip of the triangle. Whatever is at the tip of the triangle—people, this will change your life. Whatever is affecting your relationship is at the tip of the triangle and it's exactly what each person in the system needs. (Remember, everything is a system.) Why is the thing at the tip what the system needs? Why would the system need infidelity, or the valuing of work over the relationship, or drinking and going to bars excessively be the thing that the system needs in order to fix it?

Let's find out.

I asked the client: "Why did you cheat?"

He told me, "I wasn't getting attention from my wife and I started talking to my coworker who was listening to me and agreeing with me and—one thing led to another."

This question was directed at the person who was cheated on:

"Why did your partner cheat?"

Response: "I don't know."

"Okay, how did it make you feel?"

"Insecure."

"What did it do to you when you found out he was cheating?"

"It's kind of unbelievable, like surreal, because I remember thinking, *Wait, what?* It makes you doubt yourself. It takes some of your worth away."

So why do we need infidelity in the system? Because you (the partner who cheated) needed attention, you needed to be told what you wanted to hear. Because you (the partner who was cheated on) needed to reevaluate your sense of security and self-worth. Insecurity. Self-worth. If she doesn't get cheated on, she will not evaluate that. If he doesn't cheat, then he's not going to start looking at what it really is that he needs in terms of attention and who to get it from (the answer is himself, not another person).

That said, the answer is not always so clear. These are archetypal and symbolic themes. For instance, I kept attracting alcoholics as partners. (I don't drink; however, the addict archetype is ruled by Neptune, the victim and for many years I was an insufferable victim just like my mother and my partners were mirroring my shadow aspect.) The archetype of alcoholism (Neptune) is also linked to innocence and lack of clarity and lack of boundaries—and that's what kept coming up for me in relationships.

Infidelity is linked to the archetype of dishonesty and betrayal. It's the Mercury archetype. Each partner is self-betraying and being dishonest with themselves so they attract infidelity (literally or symbolically).

We haven't learned how to think symbolically, archetypally, or metaphorically so we get stuck in the details of the story. In the appendix I have provided a Descendant Shadow Archetype Keywords Chart to give you some keywords about your archetype, which is also linked to the cusp of the seventh house, the descendant in your astrological chart. You will build your entire relationship pattern on this until you do things differently, raising your consciousness in the process.

On the cusp of the seventh house, the descendant is where the sun was setting on the day of your birth. It's part of the shadow of the psyche and holds a secret that your parents "gifted" you at conception. This shadow aspect will show up in every relationship as an emotional loyalty to your parents and the union that created you. Our job through relationships is to shine light on this aspect and raise consciousness around it so as to not repeat the "sins of the Father". This is how we move the lineage forward. At the moment of conception, the relationship patterns your parents had were passed on to you as your template of how to live in relationship. Whether you knew your parents or not, whether they divorced or died, you have this programming in your psyche and you will show up in relationship according to this sign and its decans as a way to honor your parents.

The descendant is the shadow aspect in which your parents built their relationship, even if it was just a one-night stand, and is how you enter relationships, and again, unknowingly repeat the same patterns. However, the way to raise consciousness around your relationships and do things differently is to raise the vibration around the sign and archetype that dictated your parents relationship. However, the way to raise consciousness around your relationships and do things differently is to raise the vibration around the sign and decan that dictate the relationship. This is done by addressing the shadow aspects early on, or clearly during a renegotiation so there can be rules and non-negotiables written around these themes.

When shadow aspects in ourselves or in the relationship are not addressed, they become the elephant in the room. In Papua New Guinea there is a term *mokitas*, which refers to "that which everyone knows but no one speaks about." These mokitas erode relationships. These unspoken issues or shadows are held in the shadow of the seventh house cusp and decan. When we renegotiate relationships, or start new ones, this is very helpful information to use in identifying the thread, unmet needs, and non-negotiables.

IDENTIFYING THE SHADOW ARCHETYPES THROUGH OUR RELATIONSHIPS

We are symbolically and archetypally led to our partners to live out our unintegrated shadow archetypes from childhood. When I listen symbolically to clients tell me the story of how they met, their first fight, and other details about the relationship I can hear the archetype in the relationship and address shadow aspects linked to those archetypes. Most often the descendant is ruled by this archetype either in the client's astrological chart or in the combined astrological chart.

Archetypes are patterns and symbols that recur in mythology, art, and literature. The archetype that is woven into each person's own personal story reveals what issues he or she is meant to work through with their partner. And when we renegotiate the terms of our relationship, it may be that we've exhausted a particular archetype and are working through something else. Oftentimes when we end relationships, we find someone else to continue our soul's journey through these archetypes. Since we are simply a living myth based on our own origin story from conception through the age of seven, our relationships are stories that live out these archetypes so that we may heal.

There are many themes in a relationship, but they all boil down to reflect one or two of the twelve archetypes. Sally and John had a long-distance relationship. The way they met was that she had written an article for a blog and he had contacted her about the article. He pursued her for about four years until she agreed to date him. They maintained a long-distance relationship for most of that time and then she decided to leave her life in Utah to join him in Kentucky. Their first fight happened when she moved in with him and realized that he had three writing desks in what would be their master bedroom. She was a master carpenter and wanted to keep many of her tools in the bedroom as well.

This short story is loaded with symbolism about the Mercury archetype. Mercury is the messenger god and is associated with long distances, writing, and making tools. Their origin story was rooted on a mercurial thread and it was followed through until their first fight. Symbolically they met and came together as a couple to work out issues of deceit, crookedness, communication, and lies from their childhood, which was the unspoken shadow language of their parents. In my work with them, I was able to help them see this and resolve their issues sooner rather than later.

Without understanding the deeper significance of the relationship, we can spend valuable years skirting around these psychological issues that are coming up to be healed through our relationships.

Anthony and Leah met on the first day of high school, in history class. Anthony couldn't stop smiling at Leah, winking at her, singing love songs to her, and otherwise pledging his love. However, she wasn't allowed to date and repeatedly turned him down. Years later she messaged him on Facebook, and they started dating. Their first fight was when they took their first vacation and they fought about the way he had mapped out the trip. Today he works a job in which he travels a lot, taking him away from home on a regular basis.

The archetype here is the moon. Artemis is the goddess of the hunt. She rules the moon, the mother, and the family, and had one lover she accidentally killed. When Leah was in high school her parents had forbidden her to date. The moon is linked to the family, and the family, as such, is symbolized by entanglement, co-dependency, and passive-aggressive behavior. It is also about finding an identity in one's home life and nurturing and being nurtured. With Anthony being on the road so much for his job, Leah's archetypal identity with the moon was shattered and she was forced to find an identity that would be different from that of creating a home and being a wife.

In their first fight she had attempted to sabotage the relationship but she and Anthony were able to get past that and stay together. Currently they have created a home together, however, she has been forced to also find an identity that is separate and apart from marriage, motherhood, and domestic life. True to the archetype, she created a strong group of female friends and she is a volunteer at the local library.

Jasmine and Duncan met in the UK on vacation. He is British and she is American. Shortly after they fell in love she moved to Britain, and they opened a restaurant together and had children. They didn't fight for years until her first pregnancy because culturally it was inappropriate to fight. Their main archetype is Jupiter (Zeus). Long distance travel, escapism, gluttony, and avoidance behavior is typical of this archetype. Their entire marriage has been about uprooting the family to go on travel adventures and eat their way through different countries and cultures.

Both Jasmine and Duncan came from families who'd struggled with the issue of scarcity. Duncan's family went on church missions in Africa and oftentimes had no food, while Jasmine's parents lived paycheck to paycheck. Jupiter was the archetype in Jasmine and Duncan's relationship. Jupiter is the archetype of abundance (or lack thereof). Jasmine and Duncan were not consciously aware of the fact that scarcity was an issue for them and that it was linked to their unintegrated shadow. Once they addressed and integrated this they were able to enjoy their relationship and their trips more because they weren't running away from something deeper that they were scared to face.

Denise and Albert met on blind date. Albert shared how his parents fell in love—it was love at first sight—and Denise shared how her parents were still madly in love after fifty years of marriage. They started dating and were not wholly truthful about themselves. Albert would binge drink to numb his inadequacies and Denise was a medium and was scared to share this with Albert, who'd had a religious upbringing. Their first fight was when Denise felt that Albert didn't respond appropriately to an emotional meltdown she was having.

The obvious archetype here is Neptune; it rules fantasy, innocence, codependence, addiction, and spirituality. Neptune is the quintessential snow globe that they tried keeping intact by withholding information about themselves from one another. Neptune is characterized by illusion and delusion and as such, is not entirely honest. Denise's meltdown was a call for help on her part and an attempt to provoke Albert as a way of testing his love for her. This is common with this archetype because Neptune is linked to the original snow globe: the womb.

In my work with Denise and Albert, we worked on the issues of clarity and transparency and made sure that each partner felt comfortable asking the other to meet specific needs of theirs. As it turned out, Denise was very understanding of Albert's drinking and resolved to help him to stop binging. And Albert became interested in spirituality when Denise explained her mediumship practice to him. Given this, they were able to shift the vibration around the Neptune archetype—from a state of innocence to one more spiritual in nature—which reflected Denise's deeper inner knowing and intuition.

Discovering What You Need to Give Yourself

The truth is in the tip of the triangle. Any single thing that is annoying you, that is affecting you, that is bothering you, that is driving you crazy in your relationship is what you need to give to yourself. For instance, Rebecca needs to cheat on herself with herself. James needs to give attention to himself, not receive it from another person. He needs to tell himself what he needs to hear.

The tip of the triangle is symbolic of the parent you discarded or failed to integrate. It is exactly linked to what the parent did not give you. It is linked to your unmet needs from childhood. You attract the person, and these situations, to prove you are not worth getting your needs met and that your parents were right when they discarded you (Hephaestus). You create conflict (Aries) to try and get your needs met instead of meeting the needs for yourself.

That's why in this model you only get to request one need that your partner will meet for you. It is your job to meet your needs, not his or hers—nobody's but your own.

If you apply this principle to your life, your life will change. And guess what? What you find out is at the tip of the triangle and what you need to give to yourself is also what you need to give to the other person. James needed to give his wife attention and tell her what she needed to hear. Rebecca needed to take away a little bit too much of the worth that she was giving to her partner and give it to herself.

I told Rebecca, "You need to pay more attention to yourself." She had paid zero attention to herself. She neglected herself. James wanted compassion. When I asked her what *she* wanted she said "compassion." She hadn't been compassionate with herself. She was a professional bodybuilder and her hair was falling out. She was driving herself to have only 2 percent body fat and never took a day off. This equals zero compassion. Her husband wanted compassion and that tells me that's what they needed to give themselves (individually) and the relationship as well.

I'm going to tell you about the time a similar scenario happened to me.

Communication is involved in much of my work, particularly my work with spirit guides. In this, I talk a lot and perform a lot of rituals and ceremonies. One day I was doing a ceremony and I was building a small representation of a house as part of it. All of a sudden, I began to hear a voice say, "Invite your husband, invite your husband" (to participate in the ceremony). I always left him out and I didn't want to include him. As a result, I tried to ignore the voice.

He and I had had a situation where there was a third person in our marriage (not actual infidelity but there was a situation where someone had started to poke into our marriage). So, in ceremony I asked, "Why is this person showing up? Why is this person poking holes in our marriage? What is going on?" And I couldn't get an answer. At that moment, when I was building the house and I started hearing the voice, I realized "Oh, my God, the third person is at the tip of the triangle."

In my life, the third person—the "mistress"—was the spirit guides, this thing that my husband has no access to, this "third person." I had no access to the third person who was poking holes in my marriage on his side. So, if he was bringing that in, that means I was doing it too. You have to understand that if your spouse is cheating, you are cheating in another way.

Specifically, here's what happened: My husband had started going to therapy and as is common he fell for his therapist. Nothing happened, but it was a catalyst in our marriage. She was poking at my marriage and she was a third person (mistress) who I had no access to. So, I knew this was mirroring something in me. Again, he had no access to my spirit guides who poked at our marriage. Once I realized that I was creating this, he came clean, and although the marriage didn't last forever, we did work through that part of it and stayed together for another year.

In Rebecca's case, she was cheating on herself when her husband cheated on her because she was giving him the power that she needed to give to herself, the worth she needed to give to herself. When you can draw the triangle and honestly say, "This thing at the tip of the triangle, where am I doing this to myself?" you will have the answer to your relationship questions. Again, the answer is what you need to give to yourself. James needed to give himself attention and to give his wife attention. Rebecca needed to give herself some of the worth she was giving to her partner—different sides of the same coin.

If you're being cheated on, you have to ask, "Where am *I* cheating?" It doesn't matter if you ever actually acted out the behavior because once you have the thought, "the truth is in the triangle," it's as if you've actually cheated, even though technically you haven't. In esoteric circles, thoughts are considered to be energy, and if you don't act on a thought, it will simply go somewhere else.

In other words, to create an illness, an argument, or a glass breaking, all energy must materialize into something, but not acting on the thought doesn't mean you didn't have the thought. So if you think about cheating, that came from the bad buckets. You're judging betrayal, honesty, and infidelity for instance, in one of your parents, but there it is in your thoughts. The thoughts you have don't come from nothing! They are linked to the moment of conception, your bad buckets, and exactly why you don't want to integrate your parent: Because *you are them!* You judge the bad behavior in your parent, your partner, your child, and society, because it is reflective of your bad behavior too, and you need to own it to become whole. If not, you will keep creating the same situation and keep blaming it on the other. (Yet it should also be noted that there is no "other" in spirituality. We are all one.)

You will understand that what you're creating in your relationship is simply what your inner child is telling you it needs. If you give it to yourself, and you turn around and give it to your spouse, you can heal your relationship with yourself and with your partner and with your parent. In this you have hit the three points of the triangle.

So again, start by identifying the mistress. Then ask what the mistress is providing. In the case of James and Rebecca, I said to Rebecca one day, "Why did he cheat? What did the woman give him that you didn't?" "Compassion," was her reply.

I said to her, "You need to give yourself and your husband compassion," and she said, "What? He freaking cheated! What do you mean I have to be compassionate to him?" Mirror, mirror. And how do you know exactly what you need? You figure it out and define it. Make it measurable and define it. Because with a couple that's the only way because you both might have a different idea of what compassion means.

Today both people in the system are giving themselves what they need (because whatever they write and define, they're going to give it to themselves first) then they give it to the other person. That other person could not give them friendship, attention, compassion, because they're not giving themselves friendship, attention, compassion.

As soon as you recognize that it's something—as soon as you recognize that the mistress is your shadow, that you created it for a reason, and that it is something you need to work on, you begin to climb out of victim mode. No one is doing anything *to* you. You created the situation so that you can heal your childhood wound. Your partner is simply mirroring for you what you need.

I was married to a narcissist who thought he was a king and could do no wrong. I had to own my part in this story. His self-aggrandizement mirrored to me that I had low self-worth. I learned this when he treated me poorly. This was the 0 to 100, he was one extreme and I was the other. The answer for both of us was the midpoint, the 48-52. I left the marriage, but then I worked through how little self-esteem I had and how he was occupying 100% of the "self-esteem" (albeit false) in our system. Even though I left the marriage, I used the information it provided what I needed to shift to become more balanced and gain self-worth. I learned this when he treated me poorly. I'm not minimizing the earthly story of being abused or cheated on, but we have two states of being: that which reflects our animal nature and that which reflects our spiritual nature. Our animal nature will cling to being a victim of the story, and rationalize the cheating or abuse. The spiritual being, on the other hand, learns from the story. He or she admits to creating the story in order to learn something from it. Our spiritual nature gives us insights about what we need to heal. The spiritual story gets us out of victim mode, allows us to own the story, and gives us agency. You can leave the relationship if the earthly story doesn't serve you but don't waste the spiritual essence it's providing you with in order to heal your psyche. This is living symbolically and archetypally.

When you can identify and define it, you know exactly what you need to integrate. The minute you integrate it, you integrate your shadow, your bad buckets. In doing so, you've accepted that you're your parent (which is the biggest blow to accept) and all you do is become aware. If you don't want to integrate the contents of your bad buckets, that's fine. Keep cheating; I'm not going to judge you. If you want to continue to have an adult-child transaction with your partner, go right ahead.

But if you allow your better angels to prevail, your life will change because you will stop being the victim. You will take ownership. You can fix your relationship with your parent, with yourself, and you can have a healthy, loving relationship if you're willing to accept that you're allowed to, and if you give yourself the permission to do so.

Finding the Hephaestus (Innocence) and Aries (War) In Your Relationship

We briefly mentioned Hephaestus and Aries earlier and will discuss them in greater detail here. Why are Hephaestus and Aries so important? Hephaestus is an innocent, discarded, deformed god, and Aries is a god of war and conflict. We all live this out within ourselves.

There's a Native American story that I love. A grandfather is talking to his grandson and he says, "Son, there are two wolves living inside of you: a dark wolf and a light wolf."

The grandson says to his grandfather "Which one wins?"

The grandfather says, "It depends which one you feed."

Most people want to feed their light wolf but in so doing, we shouldn't negate the dark wolf, the shadow, the bad buckets. We all have a dark side. We all have a shadow. We discard the shadow but the reality is we have to feed both of them. That's where Hephaestus and Aries come into play. The wholeness comes from feeding and acknowledging the dark wolf.

Exiting the Garden

As we know, Hephaestus was discarded. He was deformed, he

was thrown out of Olympus. Up until the age of seven—because that's when our personality is developing and we're taking on the story—something about you was pointed out as being wrong. Every single one of us has this. For example, your father died and you had to assume the role of "father of the house" and you couldn't do it as well as your father because you were a six-year-old kid. Your mother told you that girls shouldn't shave their legs, but you shaved your legs behind her back and you were reprimanded. You too have some version of this story of being "kicked out" of Olympus.

Olympus is the heaven that you see as your mom and dad—again, metaphorically mom and dad. So, from this Olympus, a part of you was discarded, was kicked out. At that moment subconsciously, you decided that you were imperfect. You, at that moment, decided you were not enough.

Even "perfect" or preferred children in a family system are flawed or represent Hephaestus. You may have been the preferred child because you never gave in to the temptation to break the rules, even though you knew you had the potential to do so. Instead, you lived up to the expectations of mom and dad. You were the best student even though you wanted to throw your schoolbooks in the river. Some of us acted on a temptation as a black sheep. Others of us didn't and stayed in our lane, but still the thought was I want to do that bad thing. You didn't do it so you wouldn't be kicked out of Olympus, but your thoughts around it kicked you out by showing you that you were imperfect. Being kicked out of Olympus is a metaphor for our imperfections that begin in our thoughts. What we judge in another, especially our lover, is oftentimes that they may engage in behaviors we think about doing, but don't. It's our thoughts that we judge, the potential we have within to be imperfect, often way before our actions. Instead, you lived up to the expectations of mom and dad. You were the best student even though you wanted to throw your schoolbooks in the river. Some of us acted on a temptation as a black sheep. Others of us didn't and stayed in our lane, but still the thought was *I want to do that bad thing*. You didn't do it so you wouldn't be kicked out of Olympus, but your thoughts around it kicked you out by showing you that you were imperfect.

Every single person has this and when we are in a relationship, those discarded parts of ourselves are recognized by the other person. However, because those are subconscious shadows we don't want to be reminded of, we start the relationship with a snow globe that has a crack in it. The first fight will tell you everything about that weak spot. When you can identify how you were kicked out of Olympus, your Hephaestus, you're going to understand why you're with your chosen partner. Because that partner also has that same story—or it could be its flip side. I married the god (Ares), the guy who was put on the pedestal by his parents. Or I married the opposite side of the coin. In my story I was Hephaestus, kicked out of Olympus. My parents were in a cult and the cult-leader told my mother she needed to raise me as her own.

Two Sides but One Coin

Don't get caught up in being with someone who represents the opposite side of the story, for again, the opposite is the same. Take a coin out of your purse: there's a heads and a tails, but there's only one coin. When we do things differently, we're in a whole other paradigm, a whole other story. If not, we're still living out our parent's story, which then becomes ours. The point of enlightenment, the point of spiritual growth, the point of the mystical marriage is so we don't continue transgenerational trauma and patterns—"the sins of the father," as the Bible says. That's the goal. Dethrone your parents.

Something else to note and understand: you were kicked out of Olympus in your own head. Maybe you were literally kicked out of the house, maybe your parents died, maybe they gave you up for adoption, maybe your story is very literal, but this is figurative, metaphorical language. The subconscious forms at the moment of conception. You were already imperfect at conception because you were given a limited body at that point. The creation myth was written. However, between 0 – 7 you assumed the story with the characters and a plotline that you continue through life with.

Re-Entering the Garden

As we've learned, part of the relationship that you have with your partner is to reclaim your innocence or to return your discarded parts of Hephaestus back to Olympus. Here is another case study from my practice that will illustrate this point. Jennie, my client, called and told me that her husband was addicted to pornography and he loved video games, both of which are an escape for him.

Her escape is tucking her baby in at night. When she puts her child down for the night she stays for a few moments in her child's bed. Our children meet our needs, so her baby meets her need to be needed. She also rounds out the picture by thinking about her ex-boyfriend. So, her husband has porn and video games and she's got her daughter and her ex. Jennie and her husband are both satisfying the innocence, the fantasy, the snow globe. They are healing, albeit in a dysfunctional way, that they were kicked out of Olympus.

We must go back into the snow globe to feel whole in the psyche. This represents our return to Olympus. The first chapter of *The Seven Gates* is called "Shattering the Snow Globe of Delusion." We are all deluded that our family of origin was healthy and happy. Those who come to me waxing poetic about how idyllic and happy their childhood was are even more delusional than those of us who realize that our childhood was not idyllic because we've already found the fissure in the snow globe.

My model helps us to find the crack, shatter the snow globe, and then put the snow globe back together again with a healthier foundation and without delusion.

▶ CHAPTER 5 ◀
THAT THIRD THING

"Your absence has not taught me to be alone, it merely has shown that when together we cause a single shadow on the wall."

~ Doug Fetherling, Canadian poet and novelist

Make no mistake about it, every single one of us wants to re-enter the snow globe. Addiction, escapism, and any form of fantasy represents you trying to reclaim your innocence. *That* is going to be the mistress in your relationship. Every relationship has a mistress because every single person is intimately embedded in a triangle, therefore we must be triangulated in our relationship. Your mistress is going to tell you something about your subconscious that you need to integrate.

This "mistress" may show up as infidelity, a real male or female person—an actual third person in your relationship. Or it may show up as an addiction to just about anything. What are some things that take your partner's energy away from you and your relationship? Their friends, their car, other men/women, drugs, drinks, watching TV, for instance. It is everything they pick instead of you. Anything that is not you that takes your partner's attention away is the parent you did not integrate. That car, that videogame, that drug goes at the tip of the triangle and is labeled the mistress. The purpose of the mistress is not to cause conflict in the "WE", unless it is linked to the thread of the relationship, unmet need or non-negotiable; however, it is to provide a mirror to the "I" so that you can give yourself and the relationship something it is crying out for.

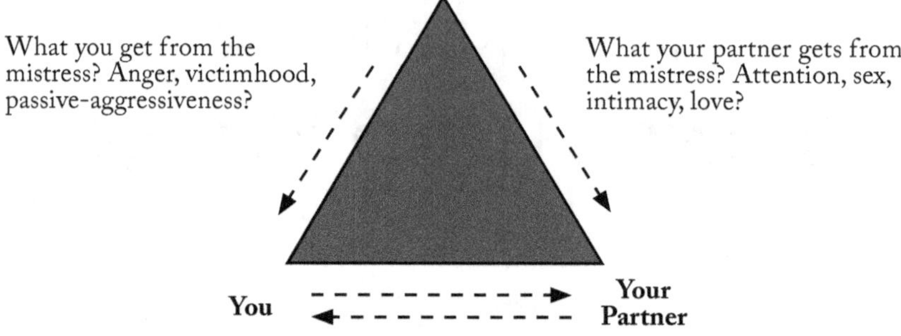

Caption: A Closer Look at "the Mistress"

"The mistress" shows up so the couple can work their bad buckets and give each other, and themselves, what each needs to be whole, to achieve the mystical marriage with Self and with the Hieros Gamos as a couple. You will have to buy in to the fact that you created the situation so you can heal. Otherwise, how do you get back into Olympus?

How do you gain the favor of your mother who threw you out because you have a clubbed foot and you're ugly and she opted for the favorite son who was brawny and gorgeous? You create a mistress to show you how.

MYTHOLOGY CAN GUIDE US

In our relationship we have to find the mistress. That's why when I'm counseling a couple the first question, I ask them is how they met; what was the fantasy that ignited the spark and drove them to unite? As we know, I then ask them what their first fight involved. The fantasy is Hephaestus, and the conflict of the first fight is represented by Aries. When you know these aspects, you can integrate them and the relationship will be healthy. That's how you rectify your own subconscious, realizing where you were thrown out of Olympus, where you were thrown out of your family— where you were discarded, literally or metaphorically.

Aries represents the ego, the need that was left unfulfilled. Where do you need to be validated? What does your partner need to bring to the relationship? Is it money? Is it conflict? Some people love to fight, and then they have great makeup sex. If you learn to unify these two aspects in yourself and then in your relationship, you can actually have a loving relationship with Self and another.

Hephaestus was thrown to the bottom of the ocean where the nymphs raised him. They taught him how to make jewelry and as a result he was a magnificent forger of fire and metal. He showed up at Olympus while Hera was having an engagement party for Aries and Aphrodite. Hera saw him and, noticing the beautiful necklace, said to him, "Son, my dear son, I love you so much. If you make me one of those jeweled necklaces, I'll give you anything you want." What do you think Hephaestus asked for? To marry Aphrodite. This is called passive-aggressive behavior. We work to prove our parents right all the time, even if it spites us. Hephaestus making Hera a necklace was his way of saying, "I told you so."

When we go through those covert power currencies, as we've learned, passive-aggression is a common feature of covert power currency. Instead of asking for what we want, we all learned as children to get our needs met in a roundabout way. You'd cry, or stay quiet, or you'd give your mother anything *she* wanted in hopes of getting your needs met. That's what that did. Hephaestus just didn't show up and say, "Mom, I'm mad at you. You hurt me. You discarded me. You threw me into the ocean." No, he showed up with a gorgeous necklace, showing it off, knowing Hera would want it.

Once Hera saw it, she said, "You can have anything you want," in exchange and he said, "I want Aphrodite," because what we all want is love. That's really what we all want. We all have four unmet needs: safety and security, protection, validation, and unconditional love. Aphrodite is a symbol of this love.

4 Unmet Needs

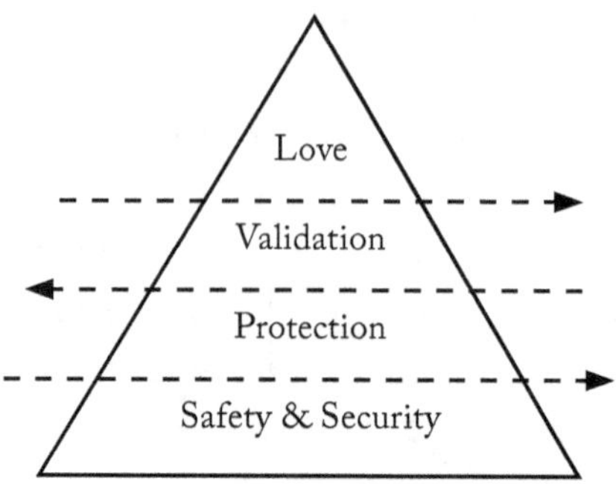

All of us lack unconditional love. The love is truly the unmet need because your parents couldn't love you unconditionally. Therefore, you were left fending for yourself as to how to manipulate the situation. As a result, we're all manipulators, hence we're all Hephaestus, wounded children, using whatever means necessary to get our parents attention to notice us and give us the love they didn't give us as children. Hephaestus used passive aggression, or codependency, or neediness—all these things that, in the therapeutic setting, we say are unhealthy in relationships. Our partner unfortunately carries the burden, as we do with them, when we haven't done deep inner shadow work, and oftentimes the price is a splitting of the couple. Ares is a metaphor for the conflict we create to hide our wound and try and get negative attention. This vicious cycle between the wound being touched upon and the conflict it creates is the mode for most relationships. Aphrodite, or love, will never come from this cycle. We need to shift the system. When couples create conflict, I have them write a conflict statement, one simple statement that sums up the conflict and assign it a conflict number from 1 to 10. Conflicts in the vicinity of 8-10 are high conflict and are linked to staying in victim. When there is no room to create something new like in an 8-10 conflict the wound is deep and oftentimes indicates the person wants to stay in victim and not look at their shadow. My goal with clients, and this book, is for you to create conflict at a lower level, say a 2-4 because then there is plenty of energy to create something new. Conflict cannot be avoided and actually serves the purpose of reminding us that we are human and flawed, so when the other person fails, we can have compassion. Conflict also feeds the need to stay in victim (child mode) a little bit, which is fine. It's a reminder that we didn't get our needs met or unconditional love in childhood and we have the right to mourn that. Conflict at a low-level like a 2-4 allows for a little victim (child mode), a reminder that self-love and getting our needs met is an inside job, and yet allows enough energy to create a new relationship and shift the system. In the workbook you will create conflict statements and assign conflict numbers to the conflicts that show up in your relationship to identify what level of conflict you create and it may link back to your wounding and whether or not you're ready to go deeper into the issues.

And Hephaestus used passive aggression, or codependency, or neediness—all these things that, in the therapeutic setting, we say are unhealthy in relationships. All of us want to go back to Olympus. All of us subconsciously want to gain the favor of our mother and father. All of us want to be allowed into the family, the snow globe, even with our defects, our bad buckets, our shadow, our club foot. And trying to get your relationship needs met in an unhealthy way is a Hephaestus-style approach. It's not a direct approach, it's not an Aries, straight-to-the-point, overt-power-currency, let's-talk-about-it approach.

Roundabout Ways We Get Our Needs Met

Codependence and addictions are two ways we seek to get our needs met. It seems ironic that an addiction would be a way to get one's needs met, but that is a tool in the covert power strategy toolbox. If you and your partner are two sides of the same coin, it makes perfect sense. If you've ever heard of Alcoholics Anonymous, you've no doubt heard of Al-Anon.

The alcoholic is the Aries archetype: straightforward and straight to the point: "I'm an addict." The person who goes to Al-Anon, on the other hand, is the Hephaestus archetype. He or she uses covert power strategies of manipulation whereby they need the alcoholic to remain an alcoholic so that they can be of service by trying to meet the needs of the alcoholic; in this, they themselves are needed.

The person who goes to Al-Anon is co-dependent; they manifest the behaviors associated with covert power currency. That's the dysfunction of the relationship from the Hephaestus aspect. It's the same reason you create your mistress. You're trying to get your needs met through that mistress. The mistress helps you stay in victim mode, proving mom and dad were right, and proving that you're unworthy and unlovable.

In terms of the individual who manifests the behaviors associated with overt power currency, often they bring the mistress into the relationship in order to keep the archetypes "in line." The conflict creator and the poor unfortunate co-dependent soul always seem to find each other.

Unpacking "the Mistress"

How do you use the mistress? Put the mistress at the top of the triangle, and ask yourself, "What am I getting from this mistress?" That mistress has a lot of information to help each person in the relationship achieve the mystical marriage with Self and in turn the Hieros Gamos with each other.

Johnny and Marta were a couple who actually attracted a real mistress, another woman, into the marriage. He cheated, and he and his wife worked through the model. They're still together as a result of integrating the symbolism of the mistress into their relationship. Johnny said the mistress provided nurturance and a maternal feeling that his wife wasn't giving him. Marta was a career professional and as such, very involved with her job. Johnny wasn't being nurtured by her; he wasn't receiving the maternal aspect that a wife can offer, and as a result, his emotional needs were not being met.

Johnny needed emotional support. His mother had abandoned him when he was four years old and the mistress was letting him know what he needed to give himself. He needed to meet his unmet needs from childhood. His inner child reached out to the mistress so that he could achieve a mystical marriage with himself and learn to meet his own needs himself. The subconscious doesn't know how to integrate the missing parent, so we create a mistress to fill the need instead.

Marta, for her part, told me that the mistress gave her space. Because her partner had a mistress, Marta had more time for herself and for the pursuit of her goals. Although she felt slighted by him for cheating, once she understood that she'd created the mistress to help her meet her needs she focused on healing herself instead of holding the space of victim.

Marta's mother had left her as a child to take care of her younger siblings. They all slept in a small room and one of her brothers molested her. She hadn't had any personal space as a child. The question to the couple "what is the mistress giving you?" allowed each person in the couple to see what they needed to give themselves individually, and then what they needed to give each other as a couple. This is the way we integrate the discarded parent, the bad buckets, with our partner and heal our childhood wounds. We recognize the discarded parts of each other and also recognize that we were drawn together because of them. My model, the Truth Is in the Triangle, is to help you stay together and complete the work you got together to do in the first place.

Daniella and her boyfriend Mark's mistress is his alarm clock. He wakes up each morning at 4:00 a.m. to go to work. It annoys her. We worked the model and I asked her what the alarm clock was giving her. "What is that alarm clock giving me? It's giving me discipline. It's getting my ass up out of bed." The alarm clock and the construct of time were a metaphor for her need to show up as an adult in her life, which she has struggled with, and to acknowl-edge her limitations. Daniella recognizes she has larger-than-life energy and needs to remember she is human. Her ego gets checked with the alarm clock, reminding her of her limitations.

The mistress helps you get your needs met. Once you identify why she is there, you can fulfill those needs for yourself. The mistress that shows up in your relationship is useful. It is not to be discarded. Just like Aphrodite needed Hephaestus and Aries to achieve love, we need to unify and integrate both Hephaestus and Aries in ourselves and in our relationships. The mistress shows up to reveal to us that facet of ourselves that has been discarded, which we need to heal.

Remember, the mistress is anything that keeps your focus away from the relationship. The purpose of the mistress, whether it's a physical person, or friends, alcohol, or an illness for instance, is to inform one as to how to integrate both Hephaestus and Aries. We call it the "mistress" because Aphrodite was a mistress to Aries. You bring a mistress into your relationship because that mistress, whatever form it takes, is there to inform you—because you were not taught appropriately by your parents—how to integrate Hep-haestus and Aries, fantasy and sex, and conflict and innocence.

A mistress exists to show you the road to self-love.

The Skinny Cows

Renegotiation can happen anytime during a threadmate rela-tionship, especially if a couple is in therapy together. However, universal law dictates that every five to seven years you will shatter the snow globe upon which the creation myth of your relationship was built. If the couple does the work, it will be rebuilt on a stron-ger foundation. Ever hear of the seven-year itch? The seven-year itch is related to a universal principle (the Principle of Rhythm) in metaphysics and a Saturn cycle in astrology. This is what I call "the skinny cows." These are the lean times, the tough times, the times of hardship and struggle.

In the story of Joseph in the Bible, the pharaoh dreamt of seven fat cows being eaten by seven skinny cows. Joseph interpreted the dream to mean that Egypt would have seven years of feast and seven years of famine. In the story, Joseph helped pharaoh and Egypt save wheat during the fat cow years so they'd have enough during the skinny cow years. This made Joseph the king of Egypt. This prophetic dream refers to the seven-year cycles in our lives that bring famine, crisis, depression, death, divorce, or any kind of limitation. These manifest as skinny cows in a couple's relationship.

You too can be the king of your kingdom (self/marriage) if you do the work during the fat cow years. However, most of us don't and so the mistress appears during the skinny cows (five- to seven-year cycles). When the skinny cows come knocking, it's an opportunity to shatter the original thread the relationship was built on and rewrite its creation story. It's an opportunity to shatter that snow globe, integrate the mistress, and build a new and healthier snow globe.

There's always going to be a mistress in your relationship because there's always a Hephaestus part of you and your partner, which wants to be integrated and return to Olympus. Everybody has an Aries archetype as well.

The Value of Conflict

This Aries archetype is in its highest consciousness as a creator or an innovator. However, with limited consciousness we live it out as conflict—either a conflict within oneself (this can be a drive but can also be self-destructive) or conflict within one's relationship. You're going to create conflict because every relationship needs to have conflict. This is according to the Zeus/Hera myth. Your conflict style will be expressed either through a covert power currency or an overt power currency. Again, each relationship will have both and this relates directly back to the unintegrated parent's bad buckets.

There's going to be a power struggle. Where did you get your fighting style? Your parents. Which parent did you get it from? The one you have the wrong alliance with is the one whose behavior you adopted as your conflict style. Your conflict style, your validation needs, your ego, your values—all of that comes from the parent who you have the wrong alliance with.

The unintegrated parent is the mistress. Her "negative" qualities are in the bad buckets, the shadow aspects you have yet to claim. People with the most "normal" type of family structure have the hardest time with this model, the wrong alliance, and the mistress, because they are the most deluded in thinking their story was a Hallmark movie. Not to say it wasn't the healthier version of the myth, but there was still dysfunction. Zeus and Hera are the king and queen of Olympus and yet they still are dysfunctional.

Every single person thinks they're screwed up because their parents didn't love them the way they should have. If you understand that *no one* has gotten their needs met, and that parents created their own subconscious imprint at conception, perhaps we would have less self-hatred and less of a chip on our shoulder.

RENEGOTIATION

How do we stay on track as we seek to develop the "I-I-WE"? One way is to realize that we have flexibility built into the model in terms of being able to renegotiate the terms of the threadmate arrangement. I'm not saying every relationship has to last forever, but it *can* because we get a chance to renegotiate it every five to seven years (or earlier if we want to). We can renegotiate those threads, the creation story, and the first fight, which, as we know, represents the crack in the snow globe.

This crack in the foundation needs to be shattered completely and rebuilt on a new shared value, a new thread, again and again every five to seven years. If the thread is romantic in nature and a couple hits some conflicts, these principles will hold true. That's the beauty of committed relationships—one is able to work the model over and over again. In this day and age most people are not doing the work together. Instead, they're checking out, leaving when the going gets rough. This model allows for a lot of conflict to occur, but all of it is in the larger interest of healing what needs to be healed so that a more balanced, stable, and evolved union is attained.

Working the Model

Identify what your Hephaestus and Aries represent. Who is who in the relationship? What parts of your psyche were discarded in childhood because they were no-goes in your family snow globe? As we suggested earlier, identify who has the covert power currency and who has the overt power currency.

Next, answer the following questions:

1. **How did you first meet?** This is your fantasy. Your creation myth. Your origin story. Your snow globe.
2. **What was your first fight?** This is the crux of every fight you will have during the five-to-seven-year period. It may seem unrelated, but it isn't.

The Importance of the Five- to Seven-Year Renegotiation

As we have established, every five to seven years of a relationship the snow globe needs to shatter. This is usually when a mistress will show up to help you integrate the shadow aspects of the parents and rebuild on a new foundation. This is the cycle of all relationships, whether you are with the same partner for thirty-five years or with multiple partners during that time.

The first fight will contain the thread of all future fights. Thus, identifying the thread early on will save you a lot of unnecessary fighting. Typically, passion and sex are initially on overdrive in new couples, usually before the first fight. Sexual energy is the Aries archetype and once it fizzles, it's turned into fighting or conflict.

The marital bed is a good place to channel Aries energy, conflicts, or the behaviors associated with our power currency. All is allowed, especially in the bedroom. Sex is usually a healthy marriage of Aries and Hephaestus, sexual energy/conflict, and fantasy, and sex is often diminished once fighting begins. At this point, we may turn inward, which causes resentment (manifesting as covert power currencies), or we fight and scream (manifesting as overt power currencies). The bedroom may be a healthy way to integrate the opposite power currency, thereby integrating the shadow. Again, if you are overtly powerful in the marriage and in life, the bedroom may provide a space where you can be more submissive or covertly powerful.

Be Clear and Be Flexible

One of the things that people have such trouble with in emotional relationships is they treat everything like a mush pot. In your job, you have a policy manual that tells you that if ABC happens, then XYZ happens. In other words, there are clearly spelled out consequences to your behavior.

Those same rules must prevail in our relationships as well. (This is step six in *The Seven Gates*.) You've got to have some rules, some non-negotiables, in your marriage, but you also, every five to seven years, during the skinny cows, get you to decide if you want out.

Alice told me she wanted to leave her husband and she'd been married for five years: right on schedule. She did not want to renegotiate. She did not want to shatter the snow globe, the origin story. She did not want to do the work to start and create a new basis for the relationship. So given that there was a fair amount of inherent conflict in the relationship, she chose to exit the marriage. There is no judgment about this. There is no judgment because she did extract the essence of what the relationship taught her. Moral of the story: Don't leave the relationship before doing the work.

You created this situation, whether it lasts for two months or twenty years, for a reason. Don't leave the situation before identifying what that reason is. You don't pick a partner because of his or her body, facial features, or hairstyle—you pick a vibration. You picked your parents for their vibration, and you pick your partner the same way. And if you don't do the work, you'll simply pick the person with the same vibration all over again—they'll just have a different face. Raise your consciousness so you can actually attract a different vibration and a different thread.

You probably didn't discuss the thread, the rules, or the non-negotiables at the outset of your initial relationship or later when you were trying to renegotiate. Most people fall in love with the fantasy, the snow globe. At a subconscious level your partner is recognizing your discarded parts, what your parents never did. However, inevitably the relationship stays in the snow globe phase and then cracks with the first fight. Without clearly establishing the non-negotiables and the thread and the unmet needs, the relationship will fail or just be a series of conflicts and honeymoons.

Don't even start the relationship if you're not on the same page of the thread, because you're going to have a crack immediately. Basically, meet the person, but immediately have the conversation: What is this? What is our thread? What is our one non-negotiable? What is the one unmet need you want me to fulfill? It's a relationship contract or a handbook like you get at work. We don't do this because we want to think it isn't a transaction—but it is. It's a very practical transaction that, if worked successfully, will save you a lot of time and heartache in the future.

Love makes it complicated because we don't want to talk about transactions in the same breath that we talk about love, but it *is* a transaction for you to get your needs met. We can eliminate so many problems and so much divorce by having these clear conversations from the get-go. A prenuptial agreement might be seen as chilling because it's a hard-boiled marriage contract when we think everything should be unicorns and rainbows. However, each party knows exactly what is expected of them in the union and clarity prevails as a result. It's infantile to think we are going to have a successful relationship on a wing and a prayer, like in fairy tales. When we gain clarity around relationships we are defying our parents and their hold over us. The good news is that if you can actually create clarity about your relationship, the hold that your parents has over you dissolves as if by magic and you are finally free to live life on your own terms.

But the sad truth is that so many of us don't want to have those clear conversations; too confrontational. We want to stay innocent; we want to stay in a passive-aggressive mode in an attempt to get our needs met. We don't want to have to say, "Look, I like a third in the bedroom. You up for it?" That's the first step in relationship, making sure there are strong channels of communication. Why even start dating her if she doesn't want a third in the bedroom? Skip right to the one who says yes. That's clarity that we have got to get to.

But Hephaestus does not represent clarity. Indeed, the word for Hephaestus is *nebulous*. He is trying to conserve the snow globe. We're all trying to conserve the snow globe. Hera threw Hephaestus out of Olympus. She said, "You're ugly. I don't like you." Again, every one of us has a crack in our family of origin, our snow globe, in our relationship, and in ourself. We all have safety/security needs because our parents were not clear. You may have gotten a B on a test in school but you got in trouble for not getting an A. Your mother may have yelled at you for something she never gave you clear guidelines about. We all come from a nebulous snow globe, with no clarity around the expectations as to how to be successful in the family.

We just have to accept this. Your snow globe is your relationship with yourself, and with your family of origin, and it needs to shatter. If it doesn't, you run the risk of living in delusion, in false innocence.

Interestingly, in some cultures of the world, women attempt to regain their innocence by replacing their hymen or tightening their vagina. This is called hymenoplasty or hymen restoration. One client had the procedure done in order to, as she said, "regain the illusion of being a virgin." These procedures are often done in the United States and other countries on women who otherwise could be killed in their own country for disgracing the family. This is because in many cultures today, a bride's virginity is considered to belong to the entire family, not just the bride. In Arabic, the *hymen* is considered to be "the face of the girl," meaning that one's identity is directly related to one's virginity and sexuality. In Egypt, this procedure of hymenoplasty or hymen restoration is available but there's a stigma attached to it.

It's also true that some women experience painful sex and/or cannot be penetrated at all. This is subconsciously a way to repair one's innocence and is called vaginismus or dyspareunia.

There are several degrees of this, ranging from mild pain to a total loss of consciousness. Renowned Dutch social scientists Charmaine Borg and Peter J. de Jong believe it is a disgust response often associated with morality. The parts of the brain related to addiction, the nucleus accumbens and the prefrontal cortex, is the part of the brain that's related to the reclamation of our innocence.

Living in delusion without cracking the snow globe is like trying to put the hymen back once you've already been penetrated with sex. We've got to get away from that and own that every system has a crack. Your relationship with yourself is a snow globe, rooted in lies and half-truths. If you actually integrate the shadow aspects of yourself you won't necessarily like what you discover. Therefore, you can judge it in your partner instead and feel superior rather than admitting you're the same.

This goes back to the power currency construct. In the renegotiation part of the relationship, the "WE," we need to re-evaluate the thread and the values the relationship is based on. Ask, what are the rules of the relationship? These have no doubt changed from the initial date. If your husband wants to watch porn and play video games, instead of creating conflict, bring it into the renegotiation. It's satisfying a fantasy, a Hephaestus aspect, so put it into the mix of what you're working on with as a couple in terms of renegotiation and creating that WE. Don't just say, "You can't play video games." That's absurd. There's room for everything in a relationship. If there are non-negotiables, then put them in your "WE."

Inclusion Rather Than Exclusion

We like to castrate ourselves. We learned from childhood to castrate parts of our psyche, our "psychological organs" as I call them. You wouldn't chop off your toes or your nose, yet we think we can castrate our tendency to be jealous, angry, or depressed. You cannot and the psyche will not let you. The repressed emotions will come out in various ways. Therefore, and again, bring them into the "WE." Honor the mistress. Honor the discarded parts of the Self.

Relationships often shatter when we move away from the original thread, the shared values that brought us together. For instance, if you do not want your partner to drink and it's a non-negotiable, and they refuse by saying it's a non-negotiable for them, you either compromise or you shatter the snow globe. Couples often stay together but violate the non-negotiables secretly all the time. They sweep the issues under the rug; they complain to their friends or their therapists. That's okay if you choose to live this way.

My model, on the other hand, is for those of you who want to be honest, who want to get out of your own way. It's for those of you who want to integrate your missing power currency and your mistress and be whole and achieve the mystical marriage with Self and your partner. If you wish to stay in victim mode, as a child, this model is not for you. You have a right to negotiate alcohol and say your spouse can drink and violate your non-negotiables, however, you don't then have a right to bitch about it. You pick how you show up in your life. That's free will. If you want to change, if you want to own your power, if you want to live your best life and be fulfilled in your significant relationships, perform these steps and I guarantee you will be successful.

You can also work the model by yourself, without your partner. You will achieve self-mastery in so doing. However, you run the risk that your partner may stay the same and not meet you in the "WE." At this point you can choose to stay in the relationship, or not. That's your choice. You don't have to break up or get divorced. However, you will have to accept that the person is not willing to do the work.

There can still be a role for your partner in your life, but it will definitely change once you put the theory and steps into effect. The key is to not leave your "I" unattended in order to overcompensate for your partner. You cannot jump in to meet their needs at the risk of negating your own.

CHAPTER 6

SHARED VALUES IN THE "I-I-WE" THREADMATE

"When you realize you want to spend the rest of your life with somebody, you want the rest of your life to start as soon as possible."

~ *When Harry Met Sally*

There are times in a relationship when couples cannot renegotiate on the new shared values the cycle is requiring. Once the snow globe is shattered, the skinny cows are in effect and the system must change. If you cannot agree on a new shared thread, shared values, non-negotiables, or a new "WE," the relationship may have reached its end. The couple decides this, no one else. However, in determining the right course of action, it's important to examine all the evidence. That's why the first fight tends to be so significant. It tells us everything about the initial crack in the snow globe. It tells us about the fighting style of the couple; who's got what power currency. It gives us a lot of invaluable information that we can use to our benefit in trying to salvage the relationship—or not.

THE FIRST FIGHT

Couples may have different ideas of what their first fight was, but most of the time they'll agree. And I'm not talking about

"Who didn't put the dish in the dishwasher?" type of silly thing. I'm talking about *the* fight. That argument, that crack in the system, that crack in the snow globe is going to keep going back to that. Oftentimes the person who starts the conflict gains the "power", whether covert or overt, in the system, and the other partner tries to assume the power with each subsequent fight. Pay attention to your patterns. Also, identify the first fight, even if it was years ago, and give it a conflict number from 1 to 10. With each subsequent fight identify if it has lowered the conflict number or if it stays the same. The ideal conflict number is between 3-5 because then it represents a balance (the 48 to 52), but it varies by couple. The crack in the snowglobe is always linked back to the first fight and every subsequent fight which is in turn linked back to your individual story of when you were kicked out of Olympus. We use conflict to get the other person (partner = parent) to meet our needs and provide unconditional love, but it is not their job. Go back to the thread, the one need and the one non-negotiable. If the conflict is addressed in this fashion any remaining inner work is yours to do in your "I". It's one of the reasons why, after fighting, people jump into bed and have makeup sex. They're trying to integrate Hephaestus and Aries. They want to reclaim the initial love they felt for one another and return to their inner Aphrodite.

Our parents also had a cracked system, whether they were married or divorced. Growing up your subconscious understood that marriage could be problematic, just as it was for Zeus and Hera, so you try to repair that broken marriage, that broken system in your own relationships as an adult. We were told subconsciously that we are here to meet our parents' needs. Whatever your parents couldn't fix in their relationship you will subconsciously sacrifice in your relationship to fix it for them. Again, this is indicated by the seventh house cusp, or descendant, in astrology. You won't veer off too much from the relationship your parents had, but you can raise consciousness around it and do things differently than they did.

WHEN YOUR PARTNER DOESN'T WANT YOU TO GO TO THERAPY

When you start therapy or do any self-help protocol, you're probably not going to receive applause from your spouse because it means that the entire family system might change and people don't like to change. This is especially true given that they're the one who aren't changing. In seeking therapy, you're trying to create a crack in the snow globe that allows for something new to be birthed. The snow globe shatters so that you can build on a new foundation.

If this is so wonderful, why doesn't your partner support your therapy?

MYTHOLOGY: ARIES AND APHRODITE

In mythology, Aries and Aphrodite are the masculine and feminine energies and represent the romantic couple. This does not have anything to do with gender or sexuality. It includes homosexual relationships as well, for this is the universal law according to the Principle of Gender. Everybody has a masculine and feminine energy (the manas prakriti) and this is what dictates sexual attraction.

Alexandre Charles Guillemot's 1827 depiction of the lovers being caught

Aries and Aphrodite had three children: Deimos, Phobos, and Harmony. *Deimos* represents a demon, *Phobos* is phobia, and *Harmony* is, well . . . harmony. As a result of the inevitable conflict in your relationship, you get to choose what level of consciousness you show up with (in the relationship) to re-establish the snow globe and the creation story.

If nothing much changes you may create Deimos, two unsatisfied people, or Phobos, fear of leaving the relationship, albeit remaining dissatisfied. However, if you work the model, you can birth Harmony, or the Hieros Gamos, from the renegotiation process.

So why does your partner fight and, more importantly, why does your partner not support you coming to therapy? This metaphor of the cracking snow globe representing the fighting energy of Aries exists to help you both create a new and better life together. Let's remember that Aries or conflict is creator energy, trying to birth something new when channeled as higher consciousness. However, when manifesting lower consciousness, it stays at the level of conflict and argument.

RESISTING CHANGE

Your partner may fight your progress because they're trying to prevent a "new life" from being birthed. A new life means a new relationship, a new marriage, a new foundation, and change. It may also mean a change in the power currency of the relationship and if your partner has the power, he or she may not want to give it up. People are afraid of change; some are even phobic about it (as represented by the daughter of Aphrodite and Aries: Phobos). It's scary to have to get to know your partner anew, start all over again, and reacquaint ourselves with one another. What if we don't like the person anymore? It's hard work, but in order to have longevity in a relationship we must birth something new. Although most people are unaware of it, their conflict is an attempt to create something new based on Harmony, or the mystical marriage.

Another child of this union, and possible rebirth of the renegotiation is Deimos. Working through our shadow brings up our demons; those we have tried to discard and pretend don't exist. Phobos may come up because your partner is scared of a new you. If you lose weight, if you go back to school, what does it mean? What about me? Where do I fit into your new paradigm? Where do I fit into your life?

All of a sudden you've got new school friends and you've got a new Weight Watchers group and you're shopping at Whole Foods. "Where do I fit into this new paradigm?" This is very scary for a partner because among other things, it may force them to examine their Deimos as well.

Your partner may not want their dirty laundry shown. The "dirty laundry" is the unconscious issues of the relationship that you're trying to bring to the conscious level. When you seek therapy, you make the unconscious conscious and perhaps reveal the truth about your passive-aggressive nature and your codependence. The false stuff that wants to stay within the confines of the snow globe will, as it bubbles to the surface of consciousness, eventually cause the snow globe to shatter. This is the Aries energy at work.

Photonis, Nemesis, Dionysus, and Deimos

In mythology there is a god of envy in love named Photonis or Nemesis and he was envious of Dionysus, the twice-born god. Your nemesis is someone who is at odds with you. This might manifest as your partner who is denying your wishes to go to therapy. However, what this really speaks to subconsciously is your own Phobos about what you will discover about yourself and the relationship once you're in therapy.

Your Deimos also appears in this scenario. What demons have you been hiding in the guise of love, where you may actually envy your partner? These are scary things to confront in a relationship and about one's own psyche. However, given that they're in the "bad buckets" (as negative personality traits), they need to be integrated for the Hieros Gamos with Self and our partner to occur.

Now let's talk about Dionysus, the transgender god in Greek mythology known as the "twice-born." He is transgender and as such symbolizes the balance between the masculine and feminine energies that we all possess. He is the whole version of the Aries and Aphrodite combination mentioned earlier.

If we work the model, we can achieve the Dionysus aspect of the relationship, the Harmony. Dionysus's birth was considered divine. Photonis was envious of this divine birth and, in the same way, Photonis represents our fear around rebirthing ourselves and our fear of upgrading our relationship to that of a mystical marriage. This envy is also based on a fear that when we do our inner work, our partner may be left behind.

It may be difficult to understand this point but the truth of it remains: our subconscious does not want us to do things differently than our parents did them. We wish to stay in child mode so as to not lose the limited version of love we received from them. Rather than seeking unconditional love, the mystical marriage, the Hieros Gamos, we sabotage due to the influence of the Phobos and Deimos constructs in our lives. In this, we keep reading from the script that we developed as a child and we fail to integrate the alienated parent.

Embodying Dionysus

Zeus was married to Hera but had an affair with the mortal Semele and became pregnant with Dionysus. Hera, knowing that Zeus's thunderbolts would destroy Semele, forced a meeting between them and they had little choice but to comply. Sure enough, the thunderbolts incinerated Semele but the quick-thinking Zeus pulled Dionysus's fetus from the remains and sewed Dionysus into his thigh, from which he was eventually born. Thus did Dionysus earn the moniker *twice-born.*

Another version of the myth posits that Dionysus was the offspring of Zeus and his daughter Persephone. He was killed by the Titans and his body was burned and eaten by them. The only thing left was his heart, which Athena saved. With this heart he was resurrected by Zeus.

Athena represents the higher consciousness of Aries. She is the goddess of war, however, she's the wisdom aspect of war, not the conflict. We need to transmute the conflict in our relationship into wisdom so that we too may be reborn. The flesh of Dionysus represents the old story of the couple. The heart represents the real essence of the couple—what remains after we change by confronting our fears and our demons. This is the love, represented by Aphrodite, which brought us together in the first place. Zeus represents our highest Self, the mystical marriage, and the thigh represents our lower human nature. The myth of Dionysus illustrates how we may experience our divinity through our humanity.

In our relationship we can experience a mystical marriage with Self, and with our partner, only after we change our level of consciousness. As Einstein said, you cannot change a problem at the same level of consciousness at which it was created. From this double birth we understand we have to kill our lower level of consciousness of the child script and bring in a new level of consciousness as the adult script. (This refers to meeting our own needs. I am now birthed in Harmony because I confronted and integrated the Phobos and the Deimos of my bad buckets that existed in my relationship.)

Athena's Heart Wisdom

Dionysius is reborn from the heart. If we really want to rebirth ourselves, if we really want to rebirth our relationship on a right foundation, it has to be from the heart. It has to be from self-love first and then agape love, love for the other. It was Athena, goddess of wisdom, who salvaged Dionysius's heart. This same wisdom that she had about his heart and the need to preserve it must be brought into *our* consciousness if we are to bring something new, a new relationship, into existence.

Through the wisdom of the heart, you can stop the power

struggle in your relationship and replace it with kindness, love, compassion, and empathy to understand that your partner is simply a mirror of yourself. He or she is also a scared little child and is worried or scared to do the work for fear of losing something—for fear of not belonging and/or for fear of recognizing his or her demons, the dark parts. The power currency is what I called "the competitive voice" in my book, *The Seven Gates*. This voice reflects the inner power struggle that we must still through self-kindness, self-love, self-compassion, and self-empathy. We are at war with Self, the inner hard edges, and only through soft corners with ourselves can we achieve the Hieros Gamos within, which will then be reflected in our partnerships.

Bring Athena, wisdom, into your own competitive voice and integrate your inner power struggle as a collaborative voice. Dionysus was reborn and considered twice-born because he represents the unification of the masculine and feminine energies, which then births the divine child. When we unify our parents (egg and sperm) and our feminine and masculine energies (within) and in our relationship, we birth our divine selves and, as well, our divine relationship.

Birthing a New Level of Consciousness

A new conception story begins with a new level of consciousness. Enjoy the new birth for a while in your new snow globe, but realize also that the cycle will start all over again with your same partner, or a new one, throughout the life cycle. Dionysus is the balance of these energies, our masculine and feminine, which makes us whole, which in part allows us to give permission to our partner to become whole and to shatter that snow globe.

The only part of Dionysus that was saved was his heart. We all need to give and receive love. So, let's work in a higher level of consciousness and meet our partner in the love. Love your partner as they want to be loved not how you want to be loved. That's the whole concept of knowing your partner's love language. That's all heart.

The symbolism of the heart in the thigh is the unification of the lower consciousness with the higher consciousness. According to the chakra system, the thigh is considered lower consciousness. The lower chakras or the human chakras in terms of the animal aspect of ourselves are the lower three chakras. The higher chakras, four, five, six, and seven reflect our humanity. That's why the symbol of the centaur, in Sagittarius, is half animal/half human. Sagittarius at its highest vibration is the sign of wisdom.

We need logic. We need the rational mind. We need ordinary consciousness, make no mistake about it. However, we also need evolved consciousness. We need heart. We need wisdom.

We need both. We combine the lower nature and the higher nature so that we can rebirth this relationship and, more importantly, ourselves.

Photonis was jealous of Dionysus because he was self-tormenting, loveless, and stung with his own poison. Fighting, bringing up the other person's dirty laundry, bringing up fights from twenty years ago is poison. You are not going to get heart and love and a healthy relationship when you're drinking poison. This is going to torment you. You're going to find yourself in a loveless relationship, first with yourself then with your spouse, if you don't integrate the exiled parent (your partner) who sits at the tip of the triangle waiting to be integrated by you.

Achieving the Hieros Gamos

Can you achieve the Hieros Gamos? I'm a believer that you can. But not every partner, not every couple wants to. That's part of knowing that some relationships are meant to end, and that's okay. Some relationships are never going to shatter that foundation of their snow globe; they're going to stay the same. This book and the model it puts forth is for those people who want to do the work, who want to integrate their parents, who want to find a healthy partner.

The answer is "yes," you can achieve the Hieros Gamos, but

it takes work. Part of that work is for you and your partner to acknowledge that the individuation process is the only way to unite the conscious and the subconscious. Individuation is when both people have a separate sense of identity and consciously show up in the world independently without being attached to the identity of another. Individuation is when aspects of our subconscious (shadow aspects, our unintegrated parent, or bad buckets) are now integrated with our conscious self.

When this happens, we've achieved the Hieros Gamos, the mystical marriage within. The earthly marriage has become mystical because it mirrors the inner work both people have done.

We are motivated subconsciously 99 percent of the time, even when choosing our partner, because we are really searching for the un-integrated parent. Thus, when we individuate, we don't need our partner to meet our needs or model the behaviors we previously failed to integrate. Because of this we become whole (individuated) and we can show up as our whole selves in the world and in our relationship.

It's the only way to integrate the light and the shadow. It's the only way to integrate the mother and the father. In order to birth something new, in order to birth the Hieros Gamos, the mystical marriage, you must birth something new in yourself. You have to allow your partner and/or yourself to marry their/your own self, to marry those energies of masculine and feminine self-love (third chakra). Then they're able, with heart, with agape love, to contribute to the marriage and make it stronger.

The Hieros Gamos, the mystical marriage to Self and then, hopefully, to one's partner, is concluded in the state of Harmony. It's not the Phobos or the Deimos. That's what most couples are in. Most couples come to me with those demons and phobias, and we want to help move them into a higher level of consciousness, into Harmony. They get to pick. Do they want to stay in their conflict, or do they want to move into Harmony with heart? If you fight your partner's progress, you're basically creating Deimos and

Phobos. You never shatter that snow globe on a new foundation.

This is dependency, this is hostility. If you don't use the skills I'm trying to impart in this book, what you could end up being is a dependent narcissist. A dependent narcissist is going to eradicate the love piece, the heart piece. Then you're just going to stay at the foundation of the triangle, which is the product of Zeus and Hera and Hephaestus and Aries. *Dependent* is a word that defines Hephaestus and *narcissist* is a word that defines Aries. A dependent narcissist is someone who may be passive-aggressive and who may be avoidant—and who may remain this way for twenty, thirty years—for the duration of their whole marriage, during which time, nothing will change.

It's Okay to Bail

Don't punish yourself for shattering the snow globe. I was talking to a client earlier who's a good example of this. He's been in his relationship for five to seven years and it's the time of his first skinny cow and he's decided to leave the marriage. So he told his wife, "I want to leave the marriage. Let's plan how this is going to go forward." They're going to stay friends, they've got small kids, they're going to coparent—all that healthy stuff. But one of the things I noticed in his language was that he wanted to punish himself because he was the one who had come to therapy and realized that this wasn't the marriage for him. It wasn't meeting his needs and he didn't want to work to save it.

This happens quite frequently. Following this, the client falls into a guilt pattern. I see this over and over again. In fact, I did it to myself. We don't fight for what we "deserve financially." We cave. For example, in the case of a separation or divorce, we may not fight for the visitation rights (to see our kids) that we deserve. Often, men will display this kind of behavior. "Oh, let her raise the kids," they'll say. "I'll see them on the weekends." What we're doing is we're punishing ourselves for actually making changes, for honoring that we want in order to grow and initiate something new.

So I said to this client, "Let me take you back to your origin story."

One of the things he said to me—and I heard the Hephaestus language immediately—was, "We were both escaping." He was escaping his single life; she was escaping her country. They came together and built the snow globe so that they could both escape. But with the first fight, the conflict, with him seeking therapy to grow and his decision to shatter the snow globe—he no longer had that need to escape. He moved through it and past it. And he does not want to rebuild on a new foundation. He wants to call it quits. This is a very typical scenario in individual and marriage and family counseling.

I said to him, "Don't pick up the pieces of the snow globe, the shattered glass, and start cutting yourself and punishing yourself because you don't want to make a new foundation, because you don't want to continue on with this person." Maybe that was the lesson to learn there. Maybe that was the mirror they both needed. We can't save the other person or the marriage because then we go into savior mode.

You can believe in the Principle of Vibration, you can believe in soulmates, you can believe in threadmates, you can believe in outgrowing someone. That's fine, but whatever it is, if you are a therapist treating such clients, don't let them punish themselves for having made this decision. You want them to show up as an adult—because they're coming from the snow globe, which represents childhood and innocence—and own their decision. This is called taking personal responsibility. There are no certainties in life, but owning your part in the creation of everything that enters your consciousness, keeps you in adult mode.

This is symbolized by Saturn, which represents adulthood, which represents limitation, which represents boundaries, which represents darkness, which represents alchemy and growing and working toward an adult Self. There is a scene from a movie that I love that illustrates this point about accepting one's adulthood. It's a film starring Owen Wilson called *No Escape*. In the movie, Wilson moves his family to Asia, and the wife is very unhappy. It's the middle of the night, she's crying in the bathroom, and he comes in to try to explain why his decision was right, and she stops him.

It was such a great depiction of her meeting her own needs and forcing him back to his "I." That wasn't a "WE" moment. She said, "I can't comfort you right now." I just thought that was so spot-on. At that moment she needed to be an adult for herself, nurture herself, meet her own needs, self-soothe. She could not take care of the partner. That's part of what the "I-I-WE" is. You're whole, they're whole, and you come together to create a new "WE." But at that moment, it was all about her (in a good way), which was absolutely appropriate. It's not uncommon to want to be a savior when your partner is in pain; however, if it is not linked to the thread and the unmet need, let them stay in their "I" and figure it out. This mirrors to you that you need to look at your savior complex in your "I". The 48-52 also refers to staying in your lane and not trying to jump in and fix, or have the other fix, the issue. In Greek mythology Hestia, goddess of the hearth couldn't leave her space at the agora. She was tasked with manning the fires. I teach clients to man their own fires, stay on their own throne, rather than jumping in and fixing it for the other person (if unrelated to the thread and unmet need) because that is simply a victim-savior complex.

Working the Model

Couples and parents and children will often ask, "How do I create this individuation or this differentiation process between my partner/my child/my parent and myself?" First and foremost, set boundaries. This is another feature of Saturn or of being an adult: have rules, have non-negotiables. This is part of creating that "WE." Establish these in the beginning. If you bowl with the guys on Tuesday night, don't give your partner Tuesday night. That's the rule book that I discuss in my first book. You need to have non-negotiables.

One person cannot meet all of your needs. Share with your

partner, share with your children, and let your children share with you, but that one person, your "partner" cannot meet all of your needs. That is not the point of a relationship. Couples learn this later on as they grow and have these skinny cow times during their relationship. It looks like they're traveling separately or they're going out with their friends too often—but that's healthy! Make friends. Have hobbies. Have other areas of interest in your life. If your relationship is it, that's trouble waiting to happen. That is a snow globe waiting to be shattered. Find other people to meet your needs.

Obviously, remember, we always try to meet our own needs first. However, as a result of living with heart, living from the fourth chakra, when we go out and have that human connection—which is part of what this whole journey is all about—we find other people to meet our needs. Maybe your old college friends meet your social and drinking needs. Maybe your book club friends meet your intellectual needs. Maybe your partner just meets your sexual needs.

That goes back to the threadmate. Go back to the thread. The thread should tell you what need your partner should fulfill for you. One need. That's it. Then, in your "I," in addition to meeting some of your own needs yourself, all of these other people are meeting your remaining needs, and in this you are complete.

CHAPTER 7

EMERGENCE OF THE DIVINE MASCULINE AND THE DIVINE FEMININE IN SOCIETY

"There is no remedy for love but to love more."

~ Henry David Thoreau

Let's go back to the Greek myths for a moment to illustrate some other seminal points. Hephaestus represents the discarded part of ourselves but he also represents innocence. So many couples have had the innocence of their relationship erode as time goes on and they must then try to reclaim it. Often it's reclaimed through a fantasy, oftentimes sexually.

The Aries archetype, which represents the warrior, sex, conflict, creator energy, is also related to sexuality. Jung, in his personality structure, said the masculine and feminine aspects of the psyche are called the anima and the animus. The anima is the female part of the male psyche, and the animus is the male part of the female psyche. Those dots in the yin-yang symbol? Those too are the anima and the animus. This has been studied and explained: we know men's bodies contain estrogen and women's bodies contain testosterone.

I had a client who one day told me she was dissatisfied with her husband. They've been married twenty-five years and she's not attracted to him anymore. As a result, she only has sex with him out of a sense of duty. This is very common. Years back, I had talked to her about the "I-I-WE" model and she had tried to get her husband interested in it but he wasn't. Cut to: Years later and she's still dissatisfied with him, so what does she do? She gets her own needs met by taking a lover. Since infidelity wasn't a non-negotiable in their marriage, it worked.

THE LAW OF OCTAVES

There's a metaphysical law that I love—my first book has a whole chapter on it—called the Principle of the Law of Octaves. It explains how people change and shift from one vibration to another. I gave you the ladder example. Let's return to it again. If you're vibrating on level D, all the other people vibrating on that same level D are, according to New Age theory, potential soulmates. What happens if you show up as an adult? What happens if you start meeting your own needs and you're advancing spiritually as a result? You move to level E now, but your spouse is still on D because he's not doing the work. This is not an easy place to be in a relationship, but some people will force things to work. It's not uncommon for couples to stay together if one's on D and one's on E because it's about the thread. This is not an easy place to be in a relationship, but some people will make things work. It's not uncommon for couples to stay together if one's on D and one's on E because it's about the thread and the shared values. Oftentimes clients will ask if they need to leave their marriage because of this work and the answer is absolutely not! You may decide to and that's a personal choice, but it is nonsense to think you need to throw away a relationship because you've integrated something your partner hasn't. It's simply a reminder of a bad bucket item you have and it no longer creates conflict.

If you are in a tough spot in your relationship, I advise you to go back to the common thread that you share with your partner. If the thread is business and the business is thriving then you should be able to stay together. If you don't have a thread to connect you anymore, the relationship may fall apart, or you can renegotiate.

In the case of the particular client who I referenced above, the common thread that she held with her husband was their children, who are now going to college and thus are out of the house. Their whole thread was raising the kids, seeing to their education, ensuring their health and well-being as they grew into adulthood. But now they—as is the case with many couples—realize they have nothing in common anymore.

Some may seek therapy at this point. Therapy often gets a bad rap; many people blame it for the break-up of the relationship. They'll say, "Therapy's bad. Therapy breaks couples up." No. If one person goes to therapy and does the work, and the other one doesn't, the relationship will fall apart. What breaks the couple up isn't therapy—again, it's the partner who's not doing the work.

Therapy may also cause conflict in the relationship. Don't get the idea that your client's family is going to be happy about them going to therapy. When one person in the system changes, the whole system has to change. This is another conflict that arises because of counseling. That's why the Aries archetype is that of a creator. It is "killing" something, shattering that snow globe, in order for something new to be penetrated—the symbol of Aries is also the symbol of the penis—and birthed.

Case Studies in a Changing Culture

Let's return to the subject of my client. She tells me she's cheating on her husband. Now, I know this client well enough to know that while having good sex is important to her, it's not the be-all and end-all of her life. She likes it and needs it in her life, but it's not at the tippy-top of her list. Some of my other couples, for example, have the BDSM[2] bed, the whips and chains, the costumes, the wigs—sex is obviously a high priority for them. For most couples, sex isn't *the* thread, but it *is* an important thread. To get Hephaestus and Aries to meet Aphrodite we need to integrate the fantasy, the sex and the penetrator, the creator aspect. Often that's satisfied by having sex and having a child. You've birthed the child, or you've birthed the business. But what happens—this is when conflict arises and a "mistress" shows up—when the fantasy is gone, when the sex is gone, when the child is gone? They need help to re-ignite the spark.

Let me digress for a moment. Robert Sternberg is an American psychologist and professor of Human Development at Cornell University. He developed a theory called the triangular theory of love. According to this theory as it pertains to interpersonal relationships, there are three components of love: intimacy, passion, and decision/commitment. Intimacy and commitment are long-term variables; the reason why couples can stay together for so many years. Passion, notoriously, fizzles out and we are constantly trying to bring it back.

Anyone who's ever been in a relationship knows after the first few months, the sex and the passion may fizzle out because intimacy and commitment kick in. The Aries archetype is also symbolic of passion. That's one of the reasons we look at the first fight. People fight and then have great sex. They shatter the snow globe then have a lot of sexual energy, creator energy. That could be the relationship style and that's how couples make it work. My client says, "I love my husband, I don't want to blow up my life, but I want good sex." She says he won't try toys or porn; he won't do *anything*.

Again, here we have the Hephaestus energy (that of the fantasy snow globe) and the Aries energy (penetration energy). These two are necessary to build the love, the intimacy, the commitment, to make something last. It's very clear to me that he feels shame about participating in the toys and the porn. "He's shaming you,

---

2 BDSM is an acronym for bondage, discipline, sadism, and masochism.

but really it's his own shame," I told her. I have to work with her to not feel guilty, to not feel shame, to ensure that she asks for what she wants sexually, to encourage it, to initiate it.

Another client of mine was a woman who, very clearly to me, wanted to castrate men. She did not want to know about men. She wanted to reach the pinnacle of success at her company—which was fine. That energy was the animus, the masculine energy that a woman has. Because of our society's high divorce rate, because women are more educated now, because women are obtaining higher-level positions, because of the deterioration of the family, because the gender roles are no longer as rigid as they used to be, women have had to assume a more "masculine" role. Their animus has grown larger. This is the masculine, Aries archetype.

The first client I mentioned was not happy with her man, but he is a good provider, husband, and father. She was very clear about not wanting to leave him even though this other guy wanted her and satisfied her sexually. She just wanted to be penetrated, to have her sexual needs met. Everything else about her marriage was fine.

The second client was completely different. She wanted to castrate men, to be in charge. I made a joke about how if a man ever offered to pay for her dinner she would laugh in his face.

Balancing the Extremes

We grew up reading fairy tales about the knight in shining armor. The knight shows up to take care of the damsel in distress, respecting her, not touching her, bringing her back home safely. No sex, no penetration, but a lot of love, compassion, empathy. A "real man." But because there is an inherent sexual dynamic between masculine and feminine, when there is a nonsexual romantic relationship, a shadow is created. The opposite of this would be the beast, the tyrant, the abuser, the aggressor, the rapist, the predator—that's more of the toxic masculine that we're trying to get rid of in society.

Societally and energetically, the burgeoning movement of a large transgender community is down to the fact that we're trying to reestablish energetically the masculine and feminine roles with a whole new paradigm. That is absolutely necessary, because the extreme toxic masculinity that has prevailed for so long needs to be deconstructed. However, this rebalancing is affecting relationships and masculine and feminine roles in that as the pendulum swings back in the direction of the feminine, men are having difficulty assuming their kingship, their warrior/masculine archetype, because they don't know which way to be. As a result, many men today feel castrated and confused.

Finding the Middle Ground

We're still trying to find a level playing field, a middle ground between these two archetypes so that they may create a healthy Aries creator archetype. Men now have a very heightened anima, feminine energy. Young women have certain rites of passage grow up—menstruation indicates that we are psychologically and biologically women, for instance. Men, on the other hand, don't have any kind of real initiation ceremony into manhood as women do. Native American cultures typically sent their young men out on vision quests, thereby marking their entry to manhood. At present there is a dearth of male initiation rites in our culture.

A lot of women today complain about the infantile men they are married to and the need to properly "raise" their men. You'll hear them say, "My husband's a baby," "My husband's a child." I saw a meme the other day: a woman is having a heart attack and she says, "Everything's fine," but a man has a little cold and he gathers all his children around him to say, "I'm dying."

Men and boys, when they have the common cold, notoriously need to be nurtured, whereas women get the same cold and move on uninterrupted. We've had this distinction forever, but it's getting more obvious today. Men are much more in touch with their feminine side. They're stay-at-home dads, changing diapers and making lunches. This is great. This is definitely a move in the right direction. The anima is heightened, but men have more estrogen and less testosterone as a result.

A lot of increasingly younger clients are using Viagra and Cialis. We're seeing the biological, psychological, mental, social, and cultural effects of this recalibration of the anima and the animus, of the sex roles. It is imperative that we talk about this in relationship. Often these things are not discussed: who's going to be the breadwinner, who's going to stay home with the kids, who's going to initiate sex.

Talk It Out with Your Partner, Not Your Therapist

These are conversations that come up in therapy because they're not talked about in the original snow globe. "We have a thread, we found each other, we love each other, we're just going to heal each other's wounds," but conflict arises because conversations about sexuality and gender roles are never had.

These need to be talked about in the discussions pertaining to the "WE" and the non-negotiables and the rule book. From the perspective of my practice, I'm seeing this more and more. Sexually dissatisfied women or women who don't want to initiate sex because they feel shame or men who have fetishes that the women don't want to participate in come to me.

That's why it's often that Aries archetype, that warrior energy, that creator energy (*creator* is synonymous with *sex* here) that causes conflict in the marriage.

I do believe that the transgender emergence is to help us balance out the extremes of our culture's sexual roles. It's important that we use the trans experience to help us redefine these traditional roles that are shifting so rapidly. Again, this may bring about problems in the marriage.

Gender Norms Get an Overhaul

I want to elaborate on this and explain why it's happening. It gets back to the combination of Hephaestus and Aries. We're redefining what love means. We're redefining shame. We're redefining sexual roles and rules. We're redefining what's allowed. I love that show *Billions*. Paul Giamatti and his wife are into bondage, discipline, sadism, and masochism (BDSM),

and he likes to be the submissive. He's running for attorney general and he basically outs himself on TV. He connected with his constituents and he won the election. In another day and age, that would never have been accepted. But he said, "Look, I'm being honest and vulnerable about myself and my sexuality," and he won.

We're in a new era! We're watching this on TV, we're talking about it with our friends. This is a huge moment in time. People are going to look back and say, "Wow, we redefined masculine and feminine roles, the anima and animus! We redefined what a relationship looks like, we're redefining glass ceilings!"

Kamala Harris is the first woman vice president of the United States. This emergence of the feminine is happening now, everywhere. Don't think that just because these shifts are happening in government doesn't mean they're not happening in people's bedrooms. The problem is that when it's brought into the bedroom, often people don't have the conversation because they probably never talked about sex with their parents. So they're shy and embarrassed, and they come to therapy and we normalize it. We say, "Oh, I have this conversation all the time with my clients."

Everything that's happening at the upper levels of government, with glass ceilings being shattered, has definitely trickled down into society. It's not only happening with the couple and their relationship. Take it a step further. It's happening with the individual—the masculine and feminine energies are being recalibrated. Whether you look at the individual, the couple, the government, society, energetically, spiritually, up and down and forward and back, it's all happening—and these changes will only continue as we step into our future and seek to redefine what it means to be human.

▶ CHAPTER 8 ◀
THE MODEL IN ACTION

"Marriages are like fingerprints; each one is different and each one is beautiful."

~ Maggie Reyes, professional life coach

In this final chapter I will present some case studies from my own practice, to further illustrate the points I've made about the I-I-WE model throughout the book.

CASE STUDY #1

Phillip and Jennifer met online, and he recalls that their first date was a "pity date." She had turned him down several times and finally she agreed to meet for dinner. They ended up having sex on that first date and then going out for several years. However, the "pity date" theme remained a thread woven throughout their relationship.

IDENTIFY THE ORIGIN STORY. IDENTIFY THE "SNOW GLOBE."	How did you meet? What fantasy is trying to be fulfilled? What discarded parts did your partner recognize?	Phillip met Jennifer online and he was immediately enamored of her. Although the first date took a while to happen and he felt it was a "pity date" he fell for her instantly and they went home together the first night.

WHAT WAS THE FIRST FIGHT ABOUT?	What was the first fight about? Identify the theme. What did the fight have to do with unmet needs from childhood? What unmet need do you most identify with?	Their first fight was when Sheryl's father died and she recalls that Phillip did not show up for her at the funeral. Phillip disagreed, saying that he escorted her family, who was in town for the funeral, to their hotel so she wouldn't have to worry about it. Regardless, she viewed this as abandonment.
IDENTIFY WHO HAD/HAS THE OVERT POWER CURRENCY. IDENTIFY WHO HAD/HAS THE COVERT POWER CURRENCY.	Whoever had/has the overt power currency needs to learn *soft corners*. Speak more softly, lower, calmer, don't yell, be centered and grounded, respond don't react. Whoever had/has the covert power currency needs to learn *hard edges*. Speak up more, say "no" more, and set firm boundaries.	Jennifer had/has the overt power. Phillip had/has the covert power. She verbally yells and speaks up while Phillip buys her gifts to try and keep the peace.
WHO ARE YOU IN WRONG ALLIANCE WITH? MOTHER OR FATHER?	You have one parent you were in wrong alliance with. This parent is usually linked to the power currency you adopted. You need to integrate the other parent. Your partner usually shows up as that unintegrated parent. The "mistress" also shows up as that unintegrated parent.	Jennifer's wrong alliance was with her father. He was overtly powerful in his community and in his relationship with Jennifer's mother. Phillip's wrong alliance was with his father who was submissive and did anything he could to keep the peace.

IDENTIFY THE THREAD OF THE RELATIONSHIP.	Why are you together? What is the focus of the relationship? Marriage, kids, money, business, sex, image, to piss off your parents, or travel, for instance? Once you identify your thread, this becomes the focus of the relationship. *The relationship is not built to meet your needs and one person cannot be everything for you.*	The thread of the relationship was identified as "having a loving relationship."

BUILD THE "I-I-WE"	In your "I" circle list the non-negotiables of the relationship. These should be just one or a few things. These are the things you will absolutely not tolerate. They are your boundaries, your "hard edges," and typically there will be a split in the relationship if they are violated. This is also a place where you may set a rule in the rule book of the relationship. For example, "I don't cook on Fridays." Your partner should populate his/her "I" circle. If your partner doesn't want to participate, that's okay. You can still do this work. In the "WE" circle, build the rules and non-negotiables of the relationship.	It was very difficult for Phillip to identify his "I." He had children, and spending time with them was important, but other than that he failed to have much of an identity. Jennifer was a marathoner, very social with her friends, an HR executive who spent a lot of time entertaining clients and traveling to see family.

IDENTIFY THE "MISTRESS"	This will eventually show up. It may be a child, an alarm clock, an addiction, or another woman. You need to integrate the mistress. Ask yourself, What is this mistress giving me? (Be honest). Your answer is what you need to give yourself so you can meet your own needs. Ask your partner, What is this mistress giving you? The answer is what your partner needs to give him/herself to meet his/her own needs. Identify what you need to give to each other based on what the mistress is giving each individual. Once the mistress is integrated it has served its purpose. *The mistress may help you see that your non-negotiables need to be renegotiated. The mistress may appear every 5 – 7 years to help shatter the original snow globe.*	The mistress in the relationship was Jennifer's gay best friend who took up most of her free time.

RENEGOTIATE THE ORIGIN STORY, FIRST FIGHT, THREAD, AND "I-I-WE."	Every 5 – 7 years (you can choose to do this sooner, however, this timeline is based on universal law and will happen right on schedule), you can renegotiate the relationship. The snow globe will shatter, creating an opportunity to build a new snow globe and a new perception of your first fight. Has your power currency changed since your original fight? Revisit the thread. It may have stayed the same or it may have changed. Update it. Did the non-negotiables change? Did the rules of the relationship change? Did your hard edges change? Did you add in soft corners? This may also be the end of the relationship.	The couple could not renegotiate as Jennifer was unwilling to do so.

COMMENTARY

Phillip and Jennifer's relationship began with a Neptune archetype. Neptune is the innocent, savior, martyr archetype that rules Pisces. There was an illusion that Jennifer was perfect. The sex they had on their first date reflects a snow globe built on codependence and a desire to be saved by the other person. The crack in the snow globe was the idea that Phillip felt pitied from the first date onward. This thread kept him feeling "less than" throughout the relationship and constantly making up to Jennifer as if to attempt to get on a pedestal beside her. There was a strong sense of inequality between them and this was reflected in their height difference as well. Jennifer was much taller than Phillip and although unspoken, height is symbolically linked to overt power and strength.

Phillip was quite codependent. He had Pisces on his descendant, and he showed up as having covert power, which can be marked by passive-aggressive, manipulative behavior. Jennifer was more overt and would yell at Phillip when he "didn't get it right!" There was a clear power struggle in the relationship.

Jennifer's gay best friend was the "mistress" in the relationship. He got to hear all of the sorrows and what Jennifer deemed the "weaknesses" of Phillip. She constantly put on her "power face" to Phillip, meaning she never let him see her vulnerabilities. He, being a sensitive person, desired to have more emotional intimacy with Jennifer, but she wouldn't let him in.

The mistress mirrored that Jennifer needed to be more sensitive to herself. She was very rigid, type A, and a perfectionist. And the mistress mirrored to Phillip that he needed to be more in tune with his emotions, rather than spending time meeting *Jennifer's* desires. He tended to spend so much time trying to please her that he neglected his own needs.

Jennifer complained that Phillip was an alcoholic, which is linked to the Neptune archetype and the Pisces descendant and a covert power style. At Jennifer's father's funeral, Phillip took her family back to their hotel without telling Jennifer. This was a case of Phillip trying to read Jennifer's mind (exhibiting codependence, which is reflective of the foundation of their snow globe). This awakened Jennifer's abandonment issues (indicated by Virgo on her descendant).

Before becoming a couple, Jennifer had individuated more than

Phillip had; she had developed more of an "I" than he had. Their relationship mirrored to him that he needed more of an identity, independent of a relationship. The origin story, as Phillip tells it, already showed the crack in the snow globe as there was an inequality woven throughout the fantasy. Phillip was living the Hephaestus myth, trying to get back to Olympus and earn his self-worth, while Jennifer was living the Aries archetype with her overt power currency. Phillip mirrored her abandonment issues, but she was not willing to integrate the shadow that these unresolved issues created and they ended up breaking up.

CASE STUDY #2

Jim and Sheryl met in college. She was an architecture major and he was a humanities major. They had similar upbringings and bonded based on the fact that they'd had similar childhoods and shared the same family values. They've been married twenty-eight years and their children had gone off to college. Jim and Sheryl found themselves in a rut, not having much in common anymore now that the kids had left. Sheryl was suffering from mild depression; Jim was still employed in the workforce. They needed a new thread, as well as to pay some attention to their unmet needs and their non-negotiables.

IDENTIFY THE ORIGIN STORY. IDENTIFY THE "SNOW GLOBE."	How did you meet? What fantasy is trying to be fulfilled? What discarded parts did your partner recognize?	They met at college and they bonded immediately about the similarity of their childhood and family experiences.

What was the first fight about?	What was the first fight about? Identify the theme. What does the fight have to do with your unmet needs from childhood? What unmet need do you most identify with?	Their first fight was when they couldn't decide how to spend their time on their family vacation.
Identify who has/had the overt power currency. Identify who has/had the covert power currency.	Whoever had/has the overt power currency needs to learn soft corners. Speak more softly, lower, calmer, don't yell, be centered and grounded, respond don't react. Whoever had/has the covert power currency needs to learn hard edges. Speak up more, say "no" more, and set firm boundaries.	Jim had/has the overt power and Sheryl had/has the covert power. Sheryl's mother was very abusive when she was young and Jim's boldness reminds her of her mother.
Who are you in wrong alliance with? Mother or father?	You have one parent you were in wrong alliance with. This parent is usually linked to the power currency you adopted. You need to integrate the other parent. Your partner usually shows up as that unintegrated parent. The "mistress" also shows up as that unintegrated parent.	Jim is in wrong alliance with his father, who was always the life of the party. His mother is a famous writer who was a recluse. Sheryl is quite reclusive as well, hiding behind her children and architectural sketches, and she rarely socializes. Sheryl is in wrong alliance with her father who was also an architect and a workaholic.

| **Identify the thread of the relationship.** | Why are you together? What is the focus of the relationship? Marriage, kids, money, business, sex, image, to piss off your parents, or travel, for instance? Once you identify your thread, this becomes the focus of the relationship. *The relationship is not built to meet your needs and one person cannot be everything for you.* | The thread was the family and the children. The twenty-eight-year relationship was built on traveling the world and living in different places so the children could have varied experiences and build their language skills. Jim and Sheryl built friendships around the children's friends and they moved around when they felt it served the children's needs. When living in Ecuador, one child was bullied so they left Ecuador to find a better fit for the child. Now both children have left for college and Jim and Sheryl have to redefine their thread. The original thread was family and kids. They decided to build wealth in real estate as their new thread. |

BUILD THE "I-I-WE"	In your "I" circle list the non-negotiables of the relationship. These should be just one or a few things. These are the things you will absolutely not tolerate. They are your boundaries, your "hard edges," and typically there will be a split in the relationship if they are violated. This is also a place where you may set a rule in the rule book of the relationship. For example, "I don't cook on Fridays." Your partner should populate his/her "I" circle. If your partner doesn't want to participate, that's okay. You can still do this work. In the "WE" circle, build the rules and non-negotiables of the relationship.	Sheryl's non-negotiable is money management. She acquired more wealth than Jim did in her position as an architect and has always had control of the finances. Jim never had interest in keeping the books but now Sheryl wants him to be involved so they can both make financial decisions together and she doesn't have to carry the weight of the bills alone, especially as they expand their real-estate holdings. Her unmet need is that he be responsible in managing the bills and the properties while she finds tenants for the rental units. Their new thread is building wealth through real-estate. This requires a paradigm shift because the default thread of "the kids" is being reprogrammed. As they work the model they are redirected to the new thread. The new snow globe is wealth and their new crack in it was a financing problem they encountered with their most recent acquisition due to a lack of funds.

IDENTIFY THE "MISTRESS"	This will eventually show up. It may be a child, an alarm clock, an addiction, or another woman. You need to integrate the mistress. Ask yourself, What is this mistress giving me? (Be honest). Your answer is what you need to give yourself so you can meet your own needs. Ask your partner, What is this mistress giving you? The answer is what your partner needs to give him/herself to meet his/her own needs. Identify what you need to give to each other based on what the mistress is giving each individual. Once the mistress is integrated it has served its purpose. *The mistress may help you see that your non-negotiables need to be renegotiated. The mistress may appear every 5 – 7 years to help shatter the original snow globe.*	The mistress in the relationship is their children. Sheryl spends a lot of time checking their status on Facebook, calling them, tracking their phones, and planning vacations around their vacation schedule. Jim is frustrated because she is spending money on the children when they'd decided to build their real estate portfolio. The time and energy Sheryl spent on chasing the children needed to be integrated as self-worth activities toward herself given that she has mild depression and has self-destructive tendencies. Jim's frustration about Sheryl's money being spent on the children is linked to his feelings of inadequacy. He also needs to work through his self-worth issues, which are linked to his financial status. His mother was very superior to and castrating of his father given that she was a famous author who made a lot of money.

Renegotiate the origin story, first fight, thread, and "I-I-we."	Every 5 – 7 years (you can choose to do this sooner, however, this timeline is based on universal law and will happen right on schedule), you can renegotiate the relationship. The snow globe will shatter, creating an opportunity to build a new snow globe and perception of your first fight. Did the power currency change? Revisit the thread. It may have stayed the same or it may have changed. Update it. Did the non-negotiables change? Did the rules of the relationship change? Did your hard edges change? Did you add in soft corners? This may also be the end of the relationship.	Jim and Sheryl renegotiated their thread, non-negotiables, and unmet needs and are currently working on building the model based on the new threads of their relationship.

COMMENTARY

This relationship started with a moon archetype, which is focused on family and children. Jim and Sheryl had a shared value system, which constituted their version of the snow globe. Their first fight pertained to a family vacation and how their time on it would be allocated. Relationships linked to the moon archetype are ruled by Cancer, which is the sign of the family and children. However, the consciousness of individuals associated with the moon archetype can be of a low level because families can be quite codependent and enmeshed, as was the case here. Fighting about time is linked to a Saturn archetype, indicating a need for boundaries and time alone to do inner work.

After twenty-eight years Jim and his wife were closing a cycle and it was time for them to address their issues of self-worth. Self-worth is related to how you spend your time, money, and resources. As stated previously, Sheryl was mildly depressed, which was taking "together time" away from the relationship. That Jim hadn't yet retired from his job reflected his desire to continue to bring home the bacon and to feel a sense of purpose and meaning in so doing. Sheryl mirrored Jim's mother who would castrate his father because she was famous and always away on a book tour (Sheryl's depression pulled her away from Jim.) Jim's un-integrated shadow was his insecurity around money, which Sheryl mirrored in her financial success as a much sought-after architect.

Their attempt to renegotiate their original understanding was an opportunity for them to shift the prevailing archetype of the moon to a Venus archetype, which rules money, love, self-worth, and real estate. Redefining a thread rooted in real estate symbolically allowed them to address these issues that needed overhauling because they were sabotaging an otherwise healthy marriage.

Case Study #3

Calvin and Jerusha met and were married in Las Vegas a week later. They've been married seven years and they say the fun is gone. They don't know how to reclaim the passion they built the relationship on.

Identify the origin story. Identify the "snow globe."	How did you meet? What fantasy is trying to be fulfilled? What did discarded parts did your partner recognize?	They met at a club and ran off to Vegas and got married a week later.

WHAT WAS THE FIRST FIGHT ABOUT?	What was the first fight? Identify the theme. What did the fight have to do with your unmet needs from childhood? What unmet need do you most identify with?	Their first fight was when they couldn't decide where to live and if they wanted kids. Jerusha had/has the overt power currency. Calvin had/has the covert power currency. Jerusha's unmet need was to be the center of attention at all times. She'd create chaos to get Calvin's attention. She'd plan trips on the fly so he could never settle down. Calvin was more covert and would drink to shut her out. He never felt he had any space or time without chaos or somewhere new to go.
IDENTIFY WHO HAS/HAD THE OVERT POWER CURRENCY. IDENTIFY WHO HAS/HAD THE COVERT POWER CURRENCY.	Whoever had/has the overt power currency needs to learn soft corners. Speak more softly, lower, calmer, don't yell, be centered and grounded, respond don't react. Whoever had/has the covert power currency needs to learn hard edges. Speak up more, say "no" more, and set firm boundaries.	Calvin's mother was bipolar and his father was always catering to her mood swings. They'd have orgies with tons of food and drink in their house and then there'd be no food for days when mom hit a low. Jerusha's dad was in the military and they moved around a lot. She learned to be very expressive because she was always the "new girl."

WHO ARE YOU IN WRONG ALLIANCE WITH? MOTHER OR FATHER?	You have one parent you were in wrong alliance with. This parent is usually linked to the power currency you adopted. You need to integrate the other parent. Your partner usually shows up as that unintegrated parent. The "mistress" also shows up as that unintegrated parent.	Calvin is in wrong alliance with his father. He is always catering to the whims of Jerusha and exhibits passive-aggressive behavior with his drinking, which mirrors the way his father would hide behind his work. Jerusha is in wrong alliance with her father who was always moving around.
IDENTIFY THE THREAD OF THE RELATIONSHIP.	Why are you together? What is the focus of the relationship? Marriage, kids, money, business, sex, image, to piss off your parents, or travel, for instance? Once you identify your thread, this becomes the focus of the relationship. *The relationship is not built to meet your needs and one person cannot be everything for you.*	The thread that Calvin and Jerusha built their relationship on was passion, excitement, innovation, and fun. Now, Calvin is tired and wants stability and Jerusha wants to continue to do fun, new, shiny things. They are renegotiating and Jerusha is discovering that Calvin cannot meet her needs and she needs to find new friends or others to go on adventures with her. Calvin needs roots and stability and he is rewriting his script to meet his own needs by creating stability in his home and not having to hide behind work or alcohol.

BUILD THE "I-I-WE"	In your "I" circle list the non-negotiables of the relationship. These should be just one or a few things. These are the things you will absolutely not tolerate. They are your boundaries, your "hard edges," and typically there will be a split in the relationship if they are violated. This is also a place where you may set a rule in the rule book of the relationship. For example, "I don't cook on Fridays." Your partner should populate his/her "I" circle. If your partner doesn't want to participate, that's okay. You can still do this work. In the "WE" circle, build the rules and non-negotiables of the relationship.	Calvin and Jerusha are realizing they are very enmeshed, chaotic, and trying to hide from real hurts endured during childhood. They both long for roots and have decided to buy a home to create more stability. The non-negotiable is not having children as they both realize they don't want children. Jerusha is going to start going on solo trips and planning more relaxing trips or couples retreats for when they travel together. Calvin is going to speak up when Jerusha's planning and adventures are too much for him. Calvin is also going to join a men's group to have some friends and time away from Jerusha that doesn't involve work or alcohol.

IDENTIFY THE "MISTRESS"	This will eventually show up. It may be a child, an alarm clock, an addiction, or another woman. You need to integrate the mistress. Ask yourself, What is this mistress giving me? (Be honest). Your answer is what you need to give yourself so you can meet your own needs. Ask your partner, What is this mistress giving you? The answer is what your partner needs to give him/herself to meet his/her own needs. Identify what you need to give to each other based on what the mistress is giving each of you. Once the mistress is integrated it has served its purpose. *The mistress may help you see that your non-negotiables need to be renegotiated. The mistress may appear every 5 – 7 years to help shatter the original snow globe.*	The mistress in this relationship is excitement and not having roots. When Calvin lives in this state of mind, he is honoring his mother's bipolar condition but abandoning himself. He needs to become calmer and find excitement within by getting to know himself and his true needs better. Jerusha is honoring her dad by moving around all the time and always being the new kid. She needs to use the mistress to meet the "new kid" inside, which is her inner child who has been abandoned by living so much on the surface of life and not having an inner life. The newness of the relationship with her inner child has started to help her settle down and desire roots. Calvin and Jerusha are giving each other a new future as homeowners and more time apart.

RENEGOTIATE THE ORIGIN STORY, FIRST FIGHT, THREAD, AND "I-I-WE."	Every 5 – 7 years (you can choose to do this sooner, however, this timeline is based on universal law and will happen right on schedule), you can renegotiate the relationship. The snow globe will shatter, creating an opportunity to build a new snow globe and perception of your first fight. Did the power currency change? Revisit the thread. It may have stayed the same or it may have changed. Update it. Did the non-negotiables change? Did the rules of the relationship change? Did your hard edges change? Did you add in soft corners? This may also be the end of the relationship.	Calvin and Jerusha have renegotiated the thread as stability, rather than excitement and instability, and their unmet need is to anchor each other by calling the other out when they see old patterns showing up and when they're feeling uprooted by the other.

COMMENTARY

Calvin and Jerusha's relationship reflects a typically chaotic, passionate, shiny and new Uranus and Mars archetypal structure. Uranus rules Aquarius and Mars rules Aries. The Aquarian archetype is linked to detachment, instability, alienation, and chaos, and the Aries archetype is linked to movement, passion, creativity, and excitement. Together these two archetypes can be explosive and fun, but as Calvin and Jerusha found out, are more than capable of burning out a relationship. Given that both Calvin's and Jerusha's childhoods lacked stability, their origin story and initial fantasy played out perfectly in their present-day scenario.

Psychologist Robert Sternberg who we mentioned earlier in the book and whose theory is the triangular theory of love, states that passion is important in relationships. However, to sustain a relationship we need commitment and intimacy. Calvin and Jerusha participated in "swinging" and other exciting sexual escapades, but they lacked the intimacy around sex, and their inability to have roots (archetypally home ownership is an attempt at having roots) demonstrated a lack of commitment to one another. They both decided that they did not want children and if at any point this changed it would be a non-negotiable and a deal breaker.

It's not uncommon for people who've had tumultuous childhoods to have fear around being a parent because you fear doing the same thing that your parents did. Calvin and Jerusha created weekly meetings to check in with one another about how they were feeling about being anchored, less enmeshed with each other, and their commitment to owning a home together.

CASE STUDY #4

Shannon and Brendan met in their mid-thirties after both had been divorced. Brendan has a three-year-old and Shannon's kids were in high school. Brendan wanted to get married, but Shannon did not. They met because Brendan had dated Shannon's sister in high school and they saw each other at a party years later and hit it off. There's a strong seductress archetype in Shannon and Brendan has a puer archetype such that he doesn't want to grow up. Shannon does not want to repeat old patterns from her previous marriage so she is being proactive about her relationship with Brendan.

IDENTIFY THE ORIGIN STORY. IDENTIFY THE "SNOW GLOBE."	How did you meet? What fantasy is trying to be fulfilled? What did discarded parts did your partner recognize?	Shannon's sister dated Brendan and years later Shannon encountered him at a party. Shannon's tendency is to be a seductress and a mistress, taking men away from other women in seeking to be the center of attention. She was a ballerina when she was younger and is accustomed to being first or chosen above other girls. This tendency seeps into her relationships. Brendan, the youngest member of his family, was continually treated as a child by them and he had to follow the family rules because of the family name, reputation, and wealth. Dating Shannon was his way of rebelling against them. Shannon's tendency was to date rich younger men who she could pull away from the societal norms they tended to follow. Brendan was seeking a mother figure given that his mother died young and has been a pedestal "ghost" figure in his family of all boys.

WHAT WAS YOUR FIRST FIGHT ABOUT?	What was the first fight about? Identify the theme. What does the fight have to do with your unmet needs from childhood? What unmet need do you most identify with?	Their first fight was whether Shannon would go to all family events with Brendan or if he would go alone at times without her.
IDENTIFY WHO HAD/HAS THE OVERT POWER CURRENCY. IDENTIFY WHO HAD/HAS THE COVERT POWER CURRENCY.	Whoever had/has the overt power currency needs to learn soft corners. Speak more softly, lower, calmer, don't yell, be centered and grounded, respond don't react. Whoever had/has the covert power currency needs to learn hard edges. Speak up more, say "no" more, and set firm boundaries.	Shannon's mother had covert power, was manipulative and cunning, and used her elevated position in society to get her way. Shannon is covert in her manipulation but overt in using her sexuality as power. Brendan is overt with his money and position, but is covert with his sexuality, playing small and behaving like a young boy.
WHO ARE YOU IN WRONG ALLIANCE WITH? MOTHER OR FATHER?	You have one parent you were in wrong alliance with. This parent is usually linked to the power currency you adopted. You need to integrate the other parent. Your partner usually shows up as that unintegrated parent. The "mistress" also shows up as that unintegrated parent.	Shannon is in wrong alliance with her father. She integrates her mother in very unhealthy ways that have previously destroyed her relationships. She wants to integrate her mother. Brendan is in wrong alliance with his dead mother who has power even though she's dead. Brendan uses this wrong alliance to play small and pretend he is insignificant, but calls the shots like his mother, behind the scenes.

IDENTIFY THE THREAD OF THE RELATIONSHIP.	Why are you together? What is the focus of the relationship? Marriage, kids, money, business, sex, image, to piss off your parents, or travel, for instance? Once you identify your thread, this becomes the focus of the relationship. *The relationship is not built to meet your needs and one person cannot be everything for you.*	The thread is that Shannon and Brendan are the "king and queen" of the prom. They are a beautiful couple with wealth and a name in the small town in which they live. They want to create scandal and have people gossip about them.
BUILD THE "I-I-WE"	In your "I" circle list the non-negotiables of the relationship. These should be just one or a few things. These are the things you will absolutely not tolerate. They are your boundaries, your "hard edges," and typically there will be a split in the relationship if they are violated. This is also a place where you may set a rule in the rule book of the relationship. For example, "I don't cook on Fridays." Your partner should populate his/her "I" circle. If your partner doesn't want to participate, that's okay. You can still do this work. In the "WE" circle, build the rules and non-negotiables of the relationship.	Shannon is very successful professionally and has a strong identity as an executive and a mother. She has strong boundaries and doesn't want Brendan in her house the nights he is with his daughter. The thread is to be the "hottest and richest couple in town" and stir things up in the community. The unmet need is that they maintain a social identity that requires them both to stay in shape, be out-and-about, and flaunt their wealth.

IDENTIFY THE "MISTRESS"	This will eventually show up. It may be a child, an alarm clock, an addiction, or another woman. You need to integrate the mistress. Ask yourself, What is this mistress giving me? (Be honest). Your answer is what you need to give yourself so you can meet your own needs. Ask your partner, What is this mistress giving you? The answer is what your partner needs to give him/herself to meet his/her own needs. Identify what you need to give to each other based on what the mistress is giving each individual. Once the mistress is integrated it has served its purpose. *The mistress may help you see that your non-negotiables need to be renegotiated. The mistress may appear every 5 – 7 years to help shatter the original snow globe.*	The mistress is a long list of lovers that Brendan previously had in town. Many of them resurface as friends, and many are business ties to his family, which he cannot sever. These lovers mirror for Shannon that she has to give herself more self-love. Her entire self-worth is based on her history growing up and as such, is rooted in an appearance, an image, and being onstage. Her mother made her feel inadequate if she didn't win first prize and get accepted to the top dancing programs. These lovers for Brendan represent Brendan setting a boundary, owning his voice, his place, and his manhood in his family. Being the youngest he never had a voice in the family business or the decision-making. Instead, he lives like a ghost and a pretty face, just like his mother. Shannon has a strong voice and boundaries that she mirrors for Brendan and he mirrors Shannon's desire to have some innocence restored as it was lost at a very young age by her mother's flaunting of her.

Renegotiate the origin story, first fight, thread, and "I-I-We."	Every 5 – 7 years (you can choose to do this sooner, however, this timeline is based on universal law and will happen right on schedule), you can renegotiate the relationship. The snow globe will shatter, creating an opportunity to build a new snow globe and perception of your first fight. Did the power currency change? Revisit the thread. It may have stayed the same or it may have changed. Update it. Did the non-negotiables change? Did the rules of the relationship change? Did your hard edges change? Did you add in soft corners? This may also be the end of the relationship.	They have begun to work the model and Shannon's clear boundaries about when Brendan stays over with or without his child have been clearly established. Brendan has stood up and asked for what he needs in terms of Shannon and a family structure. They are setting boundaries around money and how many outings a week are appropriate versus alone time for themselves, alone or together.

Commentary

Shannon and Brendan have a clear Venus (Aphrodite) archetype that they're working through in working the model. Shannon is struggling to be both a mother and a woman and Brendan is struggling with his identity as both a lover and a child (in the eyes of his family). For Shannon, their relationship awakens unmet needs from childhood where she was put on display by her mother and wasn't really allowed to *be* a child. She satisfies part of the mother archetype by caring for Brendan when he is in child mode. Shannon gets to play mother to Brendan but doesn't want to mother his child.

It is not uncommon to see a pair like this when a puer arche-type (a man or a woman who doesn't want to grow up), meets up with a strong member of the opposite sex. It's a way of staying with "mom" as a child and yet honoring the family dynamic. In Brendan's case this is especially true given that he'd lost his mother when he was quite young.

Another way that they both remain being "adult-children" is by playing house together. This is an innocent archetype built on a snow globe foundation comprised of their being key figures in their small-town bubble, having parents who paid the bills, and harboring a "prom mentality" that is linked to never really hav-ing grown up beyond high school. By being in relationship with Brendan, Shannon has stolen her sister's boyfriend—in essence, the man who broke her sister's heart. Shannon does this to "own her Venus" as the goddess of love and beauty, a construct that has played out remarkably well but one that, for the well-being of all involved, now has to change.

APPENDIX

THE TRUTH IN THE ▲
THE M-F-C TRIAD IN RELATIONSHIPS

Relationship Rules

1. Everything is a system
2. Everything is a mirror
3. We create everything
4. Your partner = parent
5. The "home" you create is the "marital home" of parents
6. Relationship is based on a creation myth
7. The creation myth will repeatedly crack the system until it either cracks or is re-established on a new myth or origin story.

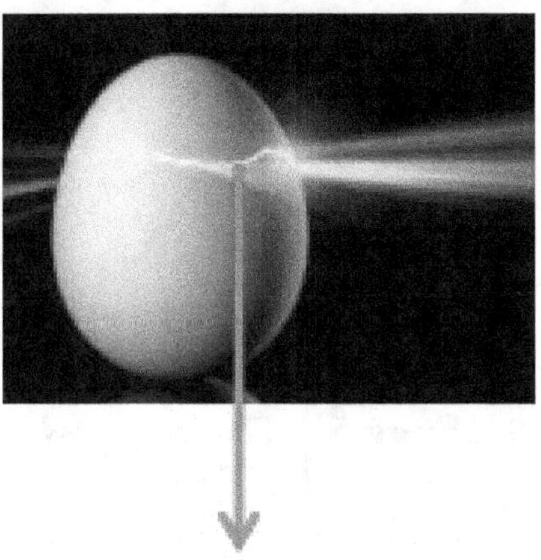

The relationships starts off with a creation Myth **based on how a couple met & their first fight.** This origin story determines all future fights and is the **"crack in the system"**

RULES TO WORK THE MODEL

1. Everything is a system.

2. There is only 100 percent in any given system, own your 48 – 52 to be whole. No more, no less.

3. You are redoing your parents' relationship. Parents = Partner with an extra *R* for "redo."

4. Your partner is your mirror, what you do not like in him/her is what you have yet to integrate in yourself (your shadow).

5. You and your partner get together because you recognize

the fragmented/dismembered parts of yourself.

6. Your origin story is how you met. This story tells the "fantasy" or delusion you're keeping alive. This is your "snow globe." If not examined, it will be why you break up.

7. Your first fight is the conflict, what you come to change in yourself via the relationship. This fight will eventually resurface to heal the delusion or the shadow aspects of Self. It is the power currency of the relationship. One person has overt power currency. The other person has covert power currency.

8. Every relationship has a mistress. The mistress shows up to help each partner integrate the unintegrated parent (shadow/bad buckets). Each partner needs to give themselves and each other what the mistress is providing.

9. Every 5 – 7 years you will shatter the origin story/snow globe and renegotiate the rules for the next 5 – 7 years and repeat this cycle throughout the relationship. If you fail to renegotiate or work the mistress/fantasy/snow globe you will break up or grow apart even if you stay "together."

10. The "I-I-WE" is a template in which to write the non-negotiables of the relationship. Each person needs to get clear on their non-negotiables and together the couple writes the non-negotiables of the relationship. This can be renegotiated.

11. The thread needs to be identified to determine the focal point of the relationship. A relationship has a focus, a thread. Identify this with your partner and stay true to its focus. This is the space where you meet each other's needs; go within and elsewhere (i.e., friends and family) to get your other needs met.

12. Write down how you met. Identify the "fantasy" in the story. This snow globe will shatter to get you out of delusion and

prompt you to do the inner work.

13. Identify your first fight. This is the crack in the snow globe that will resurface over and over to help you integrate the other's power currency. Examine every other fight and realize it always links back to that first fight. If it does not, it is not linked to the thread and is a decoy.

HIEROS GAMOS

Build the I-I-We.
What are the non-negotiables of each I and of the We?

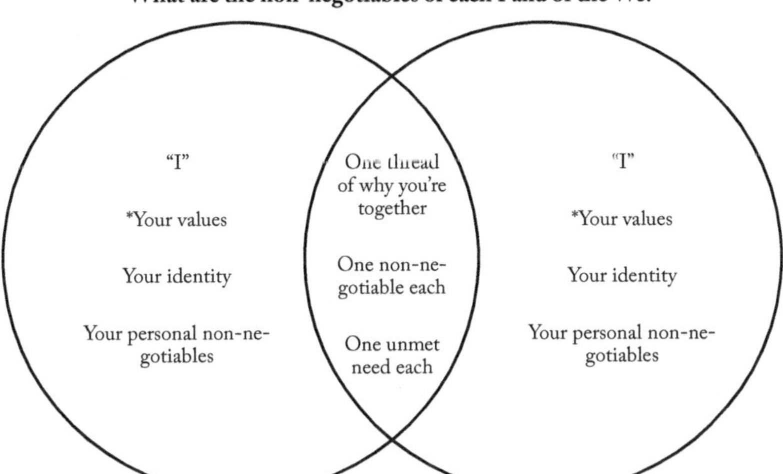

THE HIEROS GAMOS: THE MYSTICAL MARRIAGE

The Hieros Gamos is a marriage with yourself. It is the marriage of your male and female energies, making you a whole person. Oftentimes it is through a relationship that we access our mystical marriage.

To achieve a mystical marriage, draw a Vesica Piscis, two overlapping circles, and title them the "I-I-WE." The "I" is one partner, the other "I" is the second partner and the "WE" is the relationship. In your "WE" circle identify the threadmate. The threadmate is the thread that brings you together. Is it money, business, family, children, sex, image…? Be honest! The reason you are together is what you will build the relationship around and keeps you focused. Each individual "I" is where each partner writes their non-negotiables. If you bowl every Tuesday with your friends, this is your non-negotiable, don't give it away! This is your rule book, your boundaries. Every 5 – 7 years you will renegotiate these because the system will crack. Promise!

The Truth is in the Triangle Workbook

Identify the origin story. Identify the "snow globe."	How did you meet? What fantasy is trying to be fulfilled? What discarded parts did your partner recognize?	
What was your first fight about?	What was the first fight about? Identify the theme. What does the fight have to do with your unmet needs from childhood? What unmet need do you most identify with?	
Identify who had/has the overt power currency. Identify who had/has the covert power currency?	Whoever has the overt power currency needs to learn *soft corners*. Speaking more softly, lower, calmer, not yelling, being centered and grounded, responding not reacting. Whoever has the covert power currency needs to learn *hard edges*. Speak up more, say "no more," set boundaries.	

WHO ARE YOU IN WRONG ALLIANCE WITH? MOTHER OR FATHER?	You have one parent you were in wrong alliance with. This parent is usually linked to the power currency you adopted. You need to integrate the other parent. Your partner usually shows up as that unintegrated parent. The "mistress" also shows up as that unintegrated parent.	
IDENTIFY THE THREAD OF THE RELATIONSHIP.	Why are you together? What is the focus of the relationship? Marriage, kids, money, business, sex, image, to piss off your parents, or travel, for instance? Once you identify your thread, this becomes the focus of the relationship. *The relationship is not built to meet your needs and one person cannot be everything for you.*	

| **Build the "I-I-WE"** | In your "I" circle list the non-negotiables in your life. (These are different that the non-negotiables of the WE). These are linked to your values and just because of the relationship you will not violate these, These should be just one or a few. Your partner should populate his/her "I" circle. If your partner doesn't want to participate, that is okay. You can still do this work. In the "WE" circle write the thread of the relationship, list the one need you want your partner to fulfill and the one non-negotiable of the relationship. These are the things you will absolutely not tolerate. These are your boundaries, your "hard edges." These usually lead to splitting up if violated. This is also a place where you may set a rule in the rule book of the relationship. For example, "I don't cook on Fridays." Or "Tuesdays I bowl with the guys". Any conflict that arises in the relationship needs to be linked to this thread. If it is not, it is an "I" issue and you and your partner need to hold each other accountable. | |

IDENTIFY THE "MISTRESS"	This will eventually show up. It may be a child, an alarm clock, an addiction, or another woman. You need to integrate the mistress. Ask yourself, What is this mistress giving me? (Be honest). Your answer is what you need to give yourself so you can meet your own needs. Ask your partner, What is this mistress giving you? The answer is what your partner needs to give him/herself to meet his/her own needs. Identify what you need to give to each other based on what the mistress is giving each individual. Once the mistress is integrated it has served its purpose. *The mistress may help you see that your non-negotiables need to be renegotiated. The mistress may appear every 5 – 7 years to help shatter the original snow globe.*	

Renegotiate the origin story, first fight, thread, and "I-I-WE."	Every 5 – 7 years (you can choose to do this sooner, however, this timeline is based on universal law and will happen right on schedule), you can renegotiate the relationship. The snow globe will shatter, creating an opportunity to build a new snow globe and perception of your first fight. Did the power currency change? Revisit the thread. It may have stayed the same or it may have changed. Update it. Did the non-negotiables change? Did the rules of the relationship change? Did your hard edges change? Did you add in soft corners? This may also be the end of the relationship.	

THE DESCENDANT SHADOW ARCHETYPAL KEYWORDS CHART

SIGN ON DESCENDANT	SHADOW ARCHETYPE KEYWORDS
Aries	Anger, Conflict, Aggression, Overt Power
Taurus	Hoarding, Attachment, Workaholic, Vanity
Gemini	Deceit, Lie, Cheat, Steal
Cancer	Attachment, Codependent, Passive-Aggressive, Childish
Leo	Vanity, Pride, Selfish
Virgo	Judgmental, Perfectionist, Abandonment
Libra	Vanity, Superficial, Partier
Scorpio	Jealousy, Envy, Possessive
Sagittarius	Escapism, Gluttony, Infidelity
Capricorn	Workaholic, Ambitious, Greedy
Aquarius	Detached, Distanced, Cold
Pisces	Addictions, Passive-Aggressive, Codependence, Lack of Boundaries

Conflict statement. Identify the conflict in one statement.	Example. He never takes out the garbage when I ask it's like he ignores me on purpose.
Conflict number. Give the conflict a number from 1 to 10.	Example. 8
Does the conflict statement represent your mother or father? Remember this may be symbolic.	Example. Mother, she ignored me when she was with her friends.
Does this conflict relate back to the thread, unmet need and non-negotiable of the WE?	Example. Yes, the thread is owning a house together and this is housework. If the answer is no, go back to the "I" and see what it is bringing up from your wounds from childhood. This is not a relationship issue. Partners have a right to tell each other, that's an "I" issue not a "We" issue to hold them accountable with compassion. If the unmet need is "to listen when I'm working through childhood trauma" then you can offer that as well.

What don't I like about the conflict statement? Where do you currently have this behavior, have had this behavior in the past or are capable of having this behavior? This shows you that your partner is simply mirroring your shadow and it's in your mother's bad bucket. (Note: Mother is probably the exiled parent and your partner will probably mirror your mother most of the time to help you integrate her). By asking where you have had, currently have or can have this behavior you start to reduce the conflict in your body realizing it's just mirroring a part you haven't integrated. You may choose to simply become aware or start to integrate it.	Example. I have ignored friends in the past when I didn't want to go out.
After you identify the conflict is a shadow aspect of yourself and a bad bucket item does the conflict number lessen?	No. If it lessens then you're moving into adult and ready to work through the childhood wound. If it, doesn't you may still be getting your needs met by staying in child or victim mode, perhaps seeking a savior or your partner to meet your needs that are your own responsibility. If it's the latter it may be a good time to work through *The Seven Gates* workbook.

| How much energy is left over to *create from the conflict? | Example. The conflict was an 8 so there was 2 to create; however, after identifying that it was my mom it reduced to a 5 and now there's 5 to create.

*Creation is the same energy as fire, conflict, transmutation and sex. This is the Ares aspect when instead of creating conflict to get our needs met we use the energy to create something new in our relationship. |
| With the left-over energy what can you create? | Example. I will plant a tree. I will have sex. I will water the plants or walk the dog. I will bake a cake. I will buy a website domain. I will write a chapter in my book.

*Creation is anything linked to the water and earth elements and should be something observable that you're doing no matter how small.

**If the conflict is 10/10 there is nothing left to create, simply feel the emotions in your body fully and try and breathe. |

Conflict statement. Identify the conflict in one statement.	
Conflict number. Give the conflict a number from 1 to 10.	
Does the conflict statement represent your mother or father? Remember this may be symbolic.	
Does this conflict relate back to the thread, unmet need and non-negotiable of the WE?	
Where do you currently have this behavior, have had this behavior in the past or are capable of having this behavior? This shows you that your partner is simply mirroring your shadow and it's in your mother's bad bucket. (Note: Mother is probably the exiled parent and your partner will probably mirror your mother most of the time to help you integrate her). By asking where you have had, currently have or can have this behavior you start to reduce the conflict in your body realizing it's just mirroring a part you haven't integrated. You may choose to simply become aware or start to integrate it.	
After you identify the conflict is a shadow aspect of yourself and a bad bucket item does the conflict number lessen?	
How much energy is left over to *create from the conflict?	
With the left-over energy what can you create?